THE RAILWAYS OF DEVIL'S DYKE

PAUL CLARK

TURNTABLE PUBLICATIONS

SHEFFIELD

Price £2.00

MINOR RAILWAYS OF BRITAIN SERIES
SOUTH YORKSHIRE RAILWAY
THE WORLD'S OLDEST RAILWAY
THE EAST & WEST YORKSHIRE UNION RAILWAY
THE CAWOOD, WISTOW & SELBY RAILWAY
THE HECK BRIDGE & WENTBRIDGE RAILWAY
THE G.N.&L.N.W. JOINT RAILWAY
CLIFFE HILL MINERAL RAILWAY

First Published 1976
Reprinted 1983

© Turntable Publications, 1976

ISBN 0 902844 35 0

Printed by Waddington & Sons (Printers) Ltd.
Fielden Square, Todmorden, Lancs. OL14 7LE

CONTENTS

Chapter 1 — The Legend and the Hotel

Chapter 2 — The Brighton-Dyke Railway, 1887-1938
       (i) Construction
       (ii) Description of Line
       (iii) Opening
       (iv) The Brighton and Dyke Railway Company

Chapter 3 — Life of the Railway
       (i) The Halts
       (ii) Operation
       (iii) Sentinel Railbus
       (iv) Reminiscences
       (v) Closure

Chapter 4 — The Aerial Cableway

Chapter 5 — The Steep Grade Railway

Chapter 6 — Remains

Appendix   (i) — Timetable and fares, September 1887
              (ii) — Timetable and fares, June 1912
              (iii) — Timetable, November 1938
              (iv) — Logs of Sentinel Railbus trials
              (v) — Receipts, 1913

ACKNOWLEDGEMENTS

I am indebted to the following who have kindly helped me in the preparation of this book:-

J. S. Gray; M. Joly; L. Singleton; P. Hay; P. Edwards; Lens of Sutton; S. C. Nash; C. H. Attwell; D. K. Plummer; Mrs I. Stent; Mrs G. Calcutt; K. C. Leslie; L. G. Kramer; G. J. Smith of the Public Relations and Publicity Department, Waterloo Station; British Transport Historical Record Office; East Sussex County Record Office; Public Record Office; House of Lords Record Office; The British Library; Brighton and Hove Golf Club; The "Brighton Gazette"; H. C. Casserley; The Railway Correspondence and Travel Society; Ian Allan Ltd.; Department of Environment (Railway Inspectorate); and all the staff at Brighton Reference Library who have dealt with my many enquiries very efficiently.

I am also grateful to the following who either worked or knew the Dyke Railways:-

L. Budd; F. Gambling; A. Geere; W. Coney; A. C. Perryman; J. Pierce; Mrs A. Haffenden; A. Bissell; and Mrs F. Pettit.

My thanks also to Keith Gunn for his "mountaineering" at the Dyke.

CHAPTER ONE

The Legend and the Hotel

The Devil's Dyke, situated five and a half miles north-west of Brighton, is a precipitous gorge in the South Downs. The deep ravine, closed to the sea and adjacent to the Dyke Hill, which rises to 700ft above sea level, provides superb views of the surrounding countryside. In ancient times it served as a hill fort, later being used by the Romans and since time immemorial has been one of the most important tourist attractions of the South of England.

The legend from which it derives its name has played a significant part in the popularity of the Dyke. Various versions of the legend exist — even in verse — the most well-known being that of Master Cisbury Oldfirle, a schoolmaster from the neighbouring village of Poynings, who related the story of the Devil himself attempting to strike a cleft in the Downs during the night in order to let in the sea and flood the Wealden villages and churches, of whose sheltered snugness he was extremely jealous. The Devil was thwarted in his evil plan by Saint Cuthman of Steyning, who enlisted the aid of an old woman to light a taper whilst the Devil was at work. Mistaking the flickering light of the taper for the approach of daylight the Demon fled with his work half completed, leaving only his pick-axe and footprints as evidence of his presence.

Proximity to Brighton together with unparalleled views and the magnetism of the legend inevitably established the Devil's Dyke as a major tourist attraction. The views which can be had from the summit include the Isle of Wight, no less than six counties, the tower on Leith Hill in Surrey, Box Hill, Windsor Castle and, with the aid of a telescope, the village of Nettlebed in Oxfordshire and the spires of sixty churches.

In 1818 an inn, in the shape of a wooden hut which once stood on wheels near the top of Ship Street in Brighton, was erected on the Dyke Hill. This "house well stored with a profusion of refreshments" had as an early landlord one Tommy King, a noted fiddler. In 1831 a small inn was built on the site, later to become a hotel proper, and during the nineteenth century it grew to be regarded as one of the major attractions for visitors to Brighton, these visitors including at various times such notables as naturalist Gilbert White of Selborne, William IV, Queen Victoria in the early years of her reign with Prince Albert, and even Rudyard Kipling. By the 1870s it was becoming clear that the horse drawn charabanc was not the most expedient method of reaching the summit from Brighton and the coming of the railways was thus inevitable. As it turned out the Hotel was to become a major influence on the various transport systems that were to evolve and before considering the railways of the Devil's Dyke it is relevant to trace some more history of the Hotel, its proprietors, and amusements provided.

The most influential landlord was an experienced hotelier named James Henry Hubbard who bought the estate in 1892 from Thacker and Son who had been proprietors since 1835. Mr Hubbard built up the facilities at the Devil's Dyke very quickly and on Whit Monday 1893 he had no less than 30,000 visitors to his estate. He even published the "Devil's Dyke Times" with a circulation estimated at one million — such was the scale of operations! The "Devil's Dyke Times" was published, as far as can be discovered, on four occasions, costing 1d and consisting of 16 pages. The introduction to No. 4 sums up the popularity of the resort as follows:

> "What a delightful spot to spend a happy day! What pleasant memories one has of a 'day at the Dyke'! Although there are always plenty of visitors at the deservedly famous pleasure resort nearly all the year round, from Whitsuntide up till the end of September is the 'season' when the Dyke is the resort of thousands of all classes. Not only the excursionist, who comes from London to the seaside, but who never misses paying the Dyke a visit or two, but also the residents and a large number of the Society of Brighton and Hove, wend their way to the Dyke. It is quite safe to say that no pleasure resort is patronised by the residents so extensively as the Dyke."

The Hotel, according to one contemporary report, was so luxuriously equipped that it may well have been mistaken for a West End Hotel — downstairs there was a long cream and gold coffee room, holding 275 people, in which hung handsome and valuable oil paintings. Adjoining the coffee room was a cosy smoking room and upstairs was the superbly furnished dining room. The main bar, downstairs, was, according to the "Devil's Dyke Times", "equal to any West End establishment, quite eclipsing most of the bars in the Brighton Hotels."

The visitor could obtain an excellent luncheon, with the very best wines, in addition to teas and dinners. Tea could also be taken in a Bungalow, holding 200 people, at the south side of the estate — although this was principally intended for the use of ladies and children wishing to avoid the more public refreshment places near the Hotel. Among the amusements provided were a bicycle railway, swings, roundabouts, coconut shies, rocking-horses, shooting galleries, and machines to test one's strength. There was a huge wooden cannon in addition to all the sideshows. Brightonians and others could also listen to the Dyke Park Estate Brass and Reed Band which consisted of 27 musicians who delighted the visitors each Sunday with their selections of music, a special programme being prepared for Bank Holidays.

Mr Hubbard's granddaughter, Mrs G. Calcutt of Littlehampton, has in her possession a coloured London, Brighton, and South Coast Railway poster publicising the Dyke Park Estate in its heyday. This is reproduced elsewhere.

1) The Dyke Park Estate in its heyday during Mr Hubbard's regime at the turn of the century. (J. S. Gray)

2) The Dyke Hotel in the 1920s. This building was destroyed by fire in 1945. (J. S. Gray)

CHAPTER TWO

The Brighton-Dyke Railway 1887-1938

(i) Construction

The first indication of a proposal to construct a standard gauge railway was in 1872 when plans were deposited with the Clerk of the Peace on 13 November giving notice that an application was intended to be made in Parliament in the ensuing session to incorporate a Brighton and Devil's Dyke Railway Company. The objects of the proposed Company were to construct a railway commencing in the parish of Preston on the north side of the Shoreham Old Road (now known as the Old Shoreham Road). The railway was not to be connected to the main London Brighton and South Coast Brighton-Portsmouth line and would have terminated in the parish of Poynings 130 yards north west of the Hotel after climbing at 1 in 41.25 and 1 in 44. The railway was promoted as a concern independent from the L.B.S.C.R. and the Bill's future was therefore in doubt from the outset because of isolation from the main line. The Bill survived a first reading in the House of Commons on 11 February 1873 and was ordered to be committed after its second reading six days later. The order was later discharged and the Bill withdrawn through lack of support.

The scheme was revived in November 1873 when two lines were proposed simultaneously but not in competition with each other. The first would have commenced in the parish of Hove by a junction with the Brighton-Portsmouth line 1 mile 69 chains from Brighton station and would have terminated on the south side of the Dyke ravine, south west of the Hotel. The other line, known as Brighton and Devil's Dyke Railway Number 2, was to have deviated from the main Brighton-London line south of Patcham Tunnel and terminated at the same spot as proposed in the 1873 Bill. This second line would have involved a tunnel of 369 yards and a gradient of 1 in 37.3 for two miles. Whichever line became successful would have had operating powers over the L.B.S.C.R. into Brighton. Before the two Bills were submitted to Parliament, however, the promoters chose to proceed with the line commencing from a junction on the Brighton-Portsmouth line and to abandon the other undertaking. The "Brighton Gazette" optimistically reported on 22 January 1874, "As a speculation it can hardly fail to answer, and possibly the Dyke railway will be a feature in the history of Sussex."

The Bill was ordered to be committed after its second reading on 30 March 1874 but was, like the first Bill, withdrawn. According to Counsel for the Bill it was withdrawn because of the failure of negotiations between the promoters, and Lord Leconfield and the Earl of Abergavenny. These two prominent landowners in the area would have had the railway running through their land and therefore had strong opinions against the Bill generally. Lord Leconfield and the Earl of Abergavenny were called to London to put a case for the opposition to the Select Committee, an excursion involving some expense for which the two gentlemen felt entitled to claim. The

Chairman of the Committee, however, declined to award any reimbursement.

Despite these difficulties another attempt was made in the 1877 Session and this time the three promoters, William Hall, a Lancing gentleman, William Hudson, the contractor of Brighton, and William John Smith, a wine merchant of Brighton, were successful in getting the Brighton and Dyke Railway Act, dated 2 August 1877, through Parliament after much coaxing of the Committee. The Act gave the newly formed Company power to construct a railway commencing in the parish of Hove by a junction 1 mile 69 chains from Brighton station and terminating in the parish of Hangleton after 3 miles 16 chains. This railway would be known as Railway No. 1. Railway No. 2, 1 mile 50 chains in length, was to be constructed separately on the lines of the 1874 scheme and would have been connected to the southernmost line by a junction, but the Dyke railway was eventually constructed as one line, 3 miles 45 chains long.

The Capital of the Company was £72,000 and powers were given to issue debenture stock to the value of £24,000. The number of directors was to be five with a quorum of three. The Act gave permission for the L.B.S.C.R. to designate the position of the junction from the Brighton-Portsmouth line and special provision was made for the protection of the owner of the Saddlescombe estate, Lord Leconfield, who had been the stumbling block in earlier years. The Brighton and Dyke Company undertook to construct up to three bridges and a 60 yard long siding if required where the line was to pass through the estate. A sum of £3,162 was set aside as compensation for landowners whose property would be rendered less valuable by the railway. Certain portions of land required for Railway No. 2 were the property of the Crown and were sold to the Company for £100 per acre subject to an existing lease. The Act stated that the period for completion of works was to be five years from the passing of the Act and powers for compulsory purchase were not to be exercised after three years.

The original promoters were slow to undertake the construction of the line and were not helped by the unsympathetic attitudes of the directors of the L.B.S.C.R. Having lost the initiative and the services of the contractor, William Hudson, the Company was rejuvenated somewhat in 1881 when, on 18 July, new promoters succeeded in obtaining a second Act extending the time for compulsory purchase to 2 August 1883 and the time for completion to 2 August 1885. A new contractor was appointed, Henry Jackson, who was regarded as a shrewd man, and under his guidance together with the engineer, at that time A. L. Nimmo, later to stand down for Charles O. Blaber, and the enthusiastic new Chairman of the Brighton and Dyke Company, the Hon. Ashley Ponsonby, the prospects for the future of the line looked good.

In February 1882 the engineer reported to the directors that no engineering difficulties were expected to be encountered and the line should be completed within eighteen months, well within the deadline of 2 August 1885 set by the 1881 Act.

Estimates of passenger and goods traffic were calculated at this time and the optimistic prediction was that upon the opening of the line at least 273,000 passengers would make the journey each year. (At that time the population of Brighton, Hove, and Preston was about 130,000 with the number of visitors during the 9 month season amounting to between 40,000 and 50,000).

The large waggonettes at that time employed on the Brighton-Devil's Dyke road only allowed their passengers three hours there and back, and over two hours of that were consumed in travelling. The fares on ordinary days were 1s 6d and on special days 2/- as against the proposed average rail fare of less than 2/-. The fares authorised for return tickets were 2s 6d first class, 1s 8d second class, and 1s 3d third class. By the railway it was anticipated that the journey could easily be accomplished in under half an hour and passengers could return any time during the day. The prediction of Bank Holiday traffic was given by the engineer as 10,000 passengers.

The first Prospectus of the Company was issued early in 1882, giving the address as 110 Cannon Street, E.C., and stating that the Capital of £72,000 was to be issued in 7,200 Shares of £10 each. The Debentures of £24,000 would bear 4 per cent interest. The Prospectus explained that provision would be made for an intermediate station serving the districts of Saddlescombe, Poynings, and Edburton (but this was not to materialise for many years — even then it appeared in the guise of Golf Club Halt).

Agreement was reached in 1882 with the L.B.S.C.R. to work and maintain the railway and provide all necessary plant and rolling stock for 55 per cent of the gross receipts, the net balance of 45 per cent of the gross receipts to be paid over to the Dyke Company. The Directors, the Hon. Ashley Ponsonby, Frederick Edenborough, F. T. Horrocks, and Walter Otway, considered this arrangement of great importance as it secured the undertaking from any future increase in the cost of working expenses whilst ensuring an income from the day the line was opened for traffic. All profits from advertisements and other sources would belong to the Company. The L.B.S.C.R. also stipulated that when the Dyke Company's proportion of the receipts under the Agreement amounted to 7 per cent on its Share Capital, any surplus would be divided equally between the two Companies. Shareholders were promised that interest at 6 per cent would be paid by the Contractor until the line was opened.

The estimated receipts shown in the Prospectus were as follows:-

273,000 pasengers at average return fare of 1/-		£13,650
Estimated receipt for coal, goods		£ 1,500
		£15,150
Less 55 per cent as per contract with L.B.S.C.R.	£8,333	
4 per cent Debenture interest	£ 960	
Total		£ 9,293
Balance showing profit		£ 5,857

The above balance amounts to over 8 per cent upon the Share Capital. Of this, 7½ per cent would be available as dividend, the remaining ½ per cent being payable to the L.B.S.C.R.

The Prospectus optimistically stated that "probably no Town in England is extending so rapidly as Brighton, such extension developing most rapidly to the north and west. The Railway will open up a district of great salubrity and beauty, and it is fair to assume that a large residential traffic will arise on a line opening up so many new and eligible sites for building."

And so it was that the ceremony of turning the first sod was performed by Mrs Davey (wife of Alderman Davey, J.P.) as Deputy Mayoress on 2 June 1883. A small Company assembled at the Dyke and upon the sounding of a bugle made their way to a valley southwest of the Dyke Hotel. The "Brighton Gazette" reported as follows; "A small circle having been cleared a very handsome toy-sized barrow of polished oak, ornamented with silver, and a spade made in similar style, and both suitably inscribed in commemoration of the event, were presented to Mrs Davey, who dug up a piece of turf, placed it in the barrow, wheeled it to the other limit of the circle, emptied the same, and returned with the barrow behind her in what was afterwards described as a 'workmanlike' manner." The ceremony was then repeated several times to enable others present to participate as Mr Devin's band played the National Anthem. The company adjourned to a marquee for lunch after which it was optimistically envisaged that the line would be open for traffic by October 1884. The toast "Success to the Brighton and Devil's Dyke Railway" was given three times to loud applause.

Unfortunately, more difficulties were to beset the Company. Investors were slow to respond and the promoters sold out to a new Board of Directors; Major W. F. Gordon, William Stansfield, Esq., and Col. William Swynfen Jervis. The Hon. Ashley Ponsonby remained as Chairman and the new address of the Company was 20 Budge Row, Cannon Street, E.C. (Apart from a brief sojourn at 4 Great Winchester Street in 1887 the Company was to remain at the Budge Row offices until 1893). Early in 1885 a new Prospectus was issued on much the same lines as the first Prospectus of 1882, inviting applications for the remainder of the unissued Share Capital.

The Company realised that it would be impossible to complete the line by 2 August 1885 as required by the 1881 Act and took the opportunity to procure from the Board of Trade a Deviation certificate whereby the Company was empowered to deviate a portion of the railway as originally authorised and make two approach roads to the terminus. This decision was taken chiefly because of engineering difficulties which were being encountered in the last three quarters of a mile to the summit. The chalk towards the end of the line was found to be of a very hard nature and required blasting.

The Company was in a position to exercise its borrowing powers, contained in the authorising Act of 1877, when on 22 July 1885 the L.B.S.C.R. guaranteed interest at 4 per cent per annum on £24,000 to be raised as mortgages, debentures, or debenture stock. The time for completion expired less than two weeks later and ap-

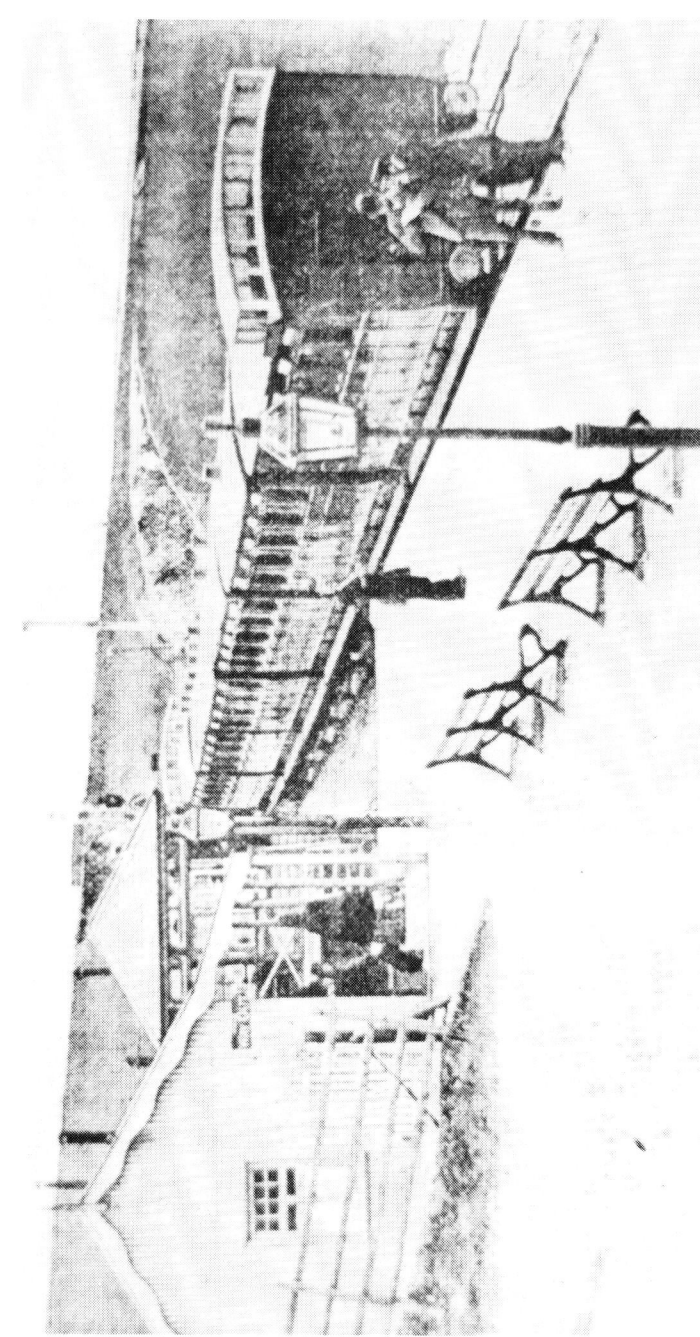

3) A set of six four-wheelers at the Dyke soon after opening. The guard stands dignified and resplendent with his patent-leather sash carrying his letter-pouch. (M. Joly)

plication was made in Parliament to extend the time yet again. This was forthcoming in the Brighton and Dyke Railway Act of 4 June 1886, when the deadline was extended to 1 June 1887.

Further difficulties were encountered in completing the line owing to the nature of the chalk and by 1 June 1887 locomotives were able to run up to 20 chains short of the terminus. Another Act of 8 August 1887 granted an extension until 1 September.

(ii) Description of the line

The single line left the Brighton-Portsmouth line half a mile beyond West Brighton station (now named Hove) at 2 miles 2 chains from Brighton, and curved away towards Hangleton through what is now Harrington's Garage. The line passed underneath the Old Shoreham Road by a girder bridge, where the gradient became 1 in 40. The climb was continuous at this gradient, with one short exception of 1 in 330, for over three miles. The average depth of cutting was 20ft and the line was of a most serpentine nature, with one curve of 13 chains radius, thereby avoiding heavy earthworks. It passed very near to Hangleton parish church, from where fine views started to be obtained of Brighton and the Channel. Where the line passed through Hangleton Farm the cutting was 40ft deep and the three overbridges and three underbridges were constructed to permit a double line. One particularly fine brick arch bridge beneath the railway was where the railway was built on a 40ft high bank. The bridge was constructed in 1883 to allow the passage of the Hangleton Road under the line.

The construction of the permanent way was similar to that of the L.B.S.C.R., the 84lb steel rails being laid with 40lb chairs and spikes and trenails on rectangular transverse creosoted sleepers. The road was well ballasted with chalk and covered with a top layer of gravel from Chichester.

The terminus was reached after a climb from the junction of 415ft. At this point the line was 501ft above sea level and 200ft below the highest point of the Downs. There was a single platform 300ft in length and 15ft wide, composed of well-bound gravel and faced with brick. The station building, situated approximately midway along the platform, was constructed of galvanised iron, the interior being matchboarded. On the north side was the ticket office and opposite were a ladies waiting room and a general waiting room. The terminus was unique in so far as there were no buffer stops at the end of the line — it being considered unnecessary in view of the chalk hillside which bordered the station.

The signalling equipment was provided by Saxby and Farmer, slotted post signals being employed initially, these later giving way to standard lower quadrants. The signal box at the Dyke was equipped with a 15-lever rocker frame and the line was worked on the train staff and ticket system. The junction signal box had a 21-lever frame.

A projected second platform, station-master's house, and goods yard siding were as yet uncompleted.

4) Dyke station in 1905. The carriage on the platform was a refreshment room run by a retired guard.
(J. S. Gray)

(iii) The opening Ceremony

On Monday 29 August the Board of Trade Inspector, Major General Hutchinson, inspected the line and declared it satisfactory for traffic. None of the bridges deflected one sixteenth of an inch when tested with a locomotive.

The formal opening took place at noon on Thursday 1 September, but in accordance with the time-table prepared (see appendix (i)) the first train ran at 8.00 am. It consisted of seven vehicles — a saloon, one first-class, and four third-class carriages, as well as a guard's van — which were drawn by "Terrier" 0-6-0T "Piccadilly". The train conveyed something like thirty passengers, among them Henry Jackson, the contractor, as well as various articles for the terminus including a clock, bell, seats, and tables.

The noon train from Brighton to the Dyke carried the Chairman of the Company, the directors, a large number of shareholders, and about one hundred influential residents of Brighton who had received invitations to attend the formal opening. The train was hauled by Class E 0-6-0T "Orleans" which was suitably decorated with bunting and miniature flags for the occasion. Upon arrival at the Dyke, at 12.20, rain had started to fall and the wife of the Chairman, the Hon. Mrs Ponsonby, declared the line open before the assemblage without further ado. She was thereupon presented with a bouquet from the daughter of the contractor and after three cheers for the railway and one cheer more for Mrs Ponsonby, the party quickly adjourned to the marquee, which had been erected behind the station, for a sumptuous luncheon, provided by Mr E. Booth, of East Street, Brighton.

The band which had been hired to entertain the guests, that of the 1st Sussex Artillery, remained outside in the rain but pity was taken upon them and before long the concert was continued from within the marquee.

Among those present were the Mayor and Mayoress of Brighton (Alderman and Mrs E. J. Reeves), Mr William Stroudley (Locomotive Engineer of the L.B.S.C.R.), and Mr John Saxby (responsible for the signalling equipment). The Hon. Ashley Ponsonby took the chair. The customary toasts followed the luncheon and these were reported in the "Brighton Gazette" on 3 September 1887 as follows; "Mr William Hall submitted 'The Army, Navy, and Volunteers.' Having taken an active part in obtaining the Parliamentary powers for the Bill for the Dyke line nearly ten years ago, he most heartily congratulated the Chairman and the members of the Board upon having brought their great work to so successful a completion — Hear, hear and applause. He hoped and trusted that in addition there might be a corresponding energy and spirit manifested by the landowners of the district, and that they might contribute to make the line pecuniarily successful. He might be permitted to put in the humorous observation that these hills in the neighbourhood of the Dyke had only been disturbed by two great works, and those were works of the spade — Laughter."

The directors, Chairman, contractor, and engineer all followed with speeches wishing the new line every success and there were many

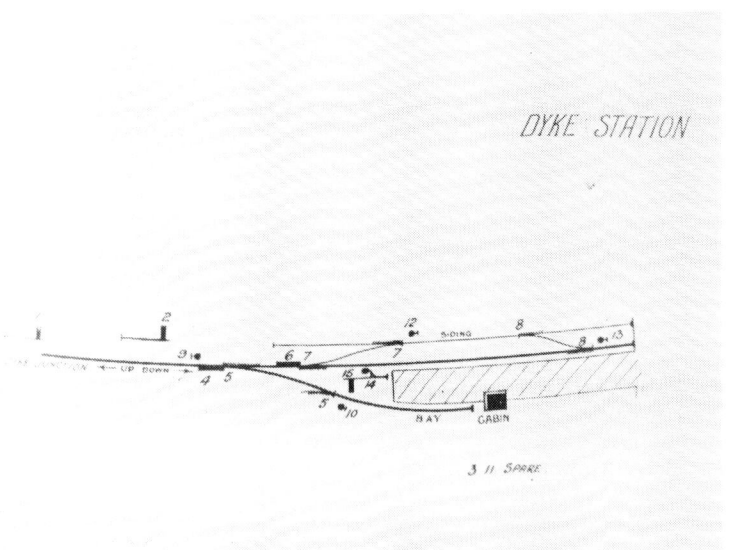

5) Track diagram — Dyke. (Courtesy P. Hay)

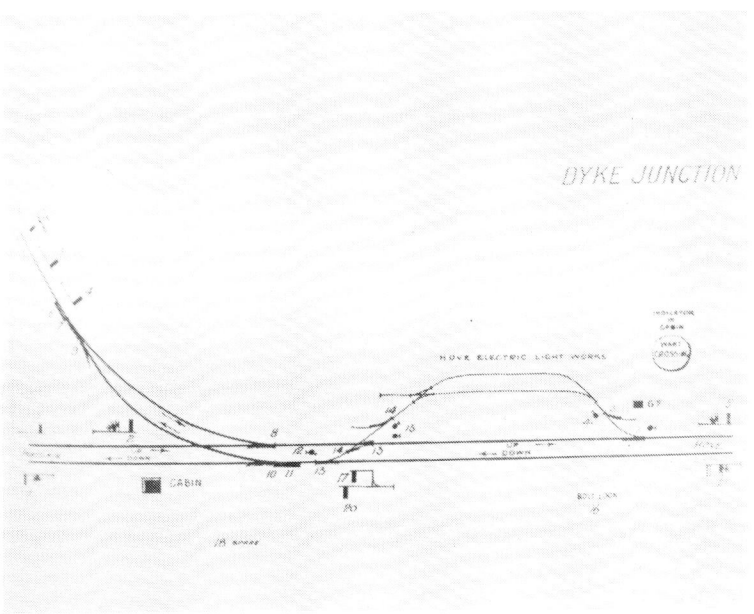

6) Track diagram — Dyke Junction (Courtesy P. Hay)

humorous references to the "Grand Old Excavator". Indeed, each succeeding speaker seemed determined not to sit down without mentioning the popular legend concerning the real "engineer" of the Dyke. Alderman Lamb remarked that the line was one of the smoothest — if not the smoothest — he had ever travelled on; it was, he said, as pleasant to ride upon as Volk's Electric Railway. Alderman Brigden remarked that there should be a spirit of "cordial reciprocity" between the two companies and he was sure that this would be forthcoming, leading to a complete success of the undertaking. As regards Mr Stroudley, "a gentleman beloved and admired by everyone who knew him", the assembly might rest assured that he would leave no stone unturned to make the new line a success. Indeed, Alderman Brigden remarked, the Dyke Railway was yet another link in the chain of attractions which Brighton possessed. These remarks prompted the band to play "Auld Lang Syne", after which Alderman Brigden sat down to vociferous cheering.

Mr Bannister, engineer of the L.B.S.C.R., humorously suggested a change of name for the locality. "What would people think of an address such as 'William Hall, Esq., Paradise, Devil's Dyke'?" Loud laughter and applause followed. His only regret was that the railway had not been carried further to the summit, to which a voice in the audience cried out, "Give it time."

Speeches by Mr Stroudley and the Mayor were followed by a witty rapport from Mr Brackstone Baker, one of the visitors. He kept the tables in a roar by discussing the claims of a certain "obscure and occult individual" to be the original proprietor of the Dyke. In the end, however, the Brighton and Dyke Railway Company had prevailed.

A telegram was read from Mr A. Sarle, General Manager of the L.B.S.C.R., who was unavoidably absent;

> "Congratulate you upon completion of Dyke Railway. Hope it will be a success. You may depend upon our Company doing all possible to make it so."

According to one of the guests at the banquet, a Mr Perry, in the course of excavation the skeleton of a lady was unearthed, and around the neck was a string of precious stones. The navvies had no respect for her bones and they were re-interred. Opinion at the time was that they were the bones of the woman who had successfully frightened away Satan. Had the remains been preserved and placed on view it was considered by the "Brighton Gazette" that "all the world would have flocked thither to look upon the remains of this extraordinary woman, which would have proved their weight in gold to the shareholders."

In the meantime the banquet was over and a few of the guests braved the rain and ventured to the summit but were glad to return to the station as the surrounding countryside was enveloped in a dense mist. The company returned to Brighton on the 5.00 pm train leaving behind them a large barrel of beer, from which the men employed in the construction of the line drank unbounded success to the promoters of the Devil's Dyke railway and their shareholders.

(iv) The Brighton and Dyke Railway Company

The new railway proved itself immenseley popular with thousands of Brightonians anxious to make the pilgrimage to the Dyke by this new means of transport. On the first Sunday of operation the traffic on the line was so great that the issue of tickets had to be temporarily suspended — an occurrence which gained mention in the "Daily Telegraph". The Sunday service was immediately judged to be insufficient to cope with the traffic and several specials were arranged. On the second Sunday, 11 September 1887, no less than 1,600 passengers were carried and throughout the rest of the month the traffic increased despite the treacherous weather. This astounding initial success of the Dyke railway at once prompted the L.B.S.C.R. to call upon the directors to enlarge the terminus to accommodate 40,000 passengers a week. By mid-1888 the directors were inviting applications for £10,000 worth of Deferred Shares still not taken up, in order to erect additional more substantial station buildings, a station-master's house, refreshment rooms, and an increase in sidings at the Dyke.

Proposals to build a station at Hangleton and extend the line to Henfield were first discussed when the line opened but no more was to be heard of these schemes.

The first meeting of the shareholders was held on 24 October 1888 when the Chairman, the Hon. Ashley Ponsonby, made a statement reported by Bradshaw's Shareholders' Guide and Manual for 1890 as follows;

"The result for the half-year ended 30 June showed that the Company had carried 48,953 passengers, which, with other receipts, made a total revenue from 1 January to 30 June of £1,103, and for the three months since — July, August, September — the number of passengers carried were 77,262, as against the 48,953 carried during the whole of the previous six months. After paying interest of £480 on debenture stock they were not in a position to pay the dividend of 5 per cent on the preference shares due on 1 July, but judging by the first year's receipts, and the completion of the railway stations and their adjuncts, next year the preference shareholders would receive their dividend in full, and probably a small dividend for the ordinary shareholders. The Brighton Company had agreed to work their railway at the rate of 55 per cent of the gross receipts, and to provide rolling stock, staff, and to keep in repair the stations, so that they would receive 45 per cent of the gross receipts free of all charge. Negotiations were proceeding with the Brighton Company for the rebate of charges made by them for mileage from Brighton Station to the junction with the Dyke Railway, and a claim for percentage on through passenger traffic."

During the first twelve months of operation, a total of 159,500 passengers was carried which was some way below the estimate of "at least 273,000" made in 1882. Although the inclement weather of 1888 could have had some effect on this low figure the first signs of trouble were apparent, and the Hon. Ashley Ponsonby and his directors must have been asking themselves whether the novelty of the Dyke railway had worn off already.

At a special general meeting, held on 23 December 1889, a scheme of arrangement between the Company and their creditors was passed. This stated that after much anxious consideration the directors decided to attempt raising funds by the issue of £10,000 worth of "B" debentures bearing interest at 5 per cent and ranking immediately after the existing debenture capital of £24,000, in order to complete the works, and to pay off the Company's liabilities to the L.B.S.C.R., and others, and so place the line on a more satisfactory working basis. The liabilities of the Company were as follows;

1 — £1,582 — Owing to L.B.S.C.R. in respect of interest paid by them upon debenture stock of the Company under the guarantee agreement of 30 July 1885, and in respect of necessary works undertaken by them for the improvement of the line.

2 — £2,000 — Payment under a Lloyd's bond for that amount given in respect of a loan from the Company's bankers, Messrs. Glyn, Mills, Currie, and Co.

3 — £2,155 — Owing to the Company's solicitors, Powell and Rogers of the Strand, London, for professional costs and disbursements up to December 1887 and a further amount since that date of which particulars were not available.

4 — £3,230 — Required for erecting permanent station accommodation.

£8,967

Despite these liabilities the directors reported to the shareholders that traffic had increased satisfactorily during 1892 and that the new goods siding completed in that year would encourage a steady goods traffic in addition to providing a means to deal with extra traffic on Bank Holidays and other busy occasions. Indeed, on Bank Holidays the railway was taxed to the utmost — especially in 1893 when a record 30,000 peole made their way to the Dyke by road, foot, and rail.

The issue of "B" debentures, however, went badly and judging by the summary of capital of the Company published in Bradshaw's Shareholders' Guide and Manual for the half year ended 30 June 1894 it was not possible to pay off the creditors;

Amount expended £88,562

Receipts;

2,212 Ordinary Shares of £10 each	£22,030
4,988 Preferred half Shares of £5 each	£24,940
4,988 Deferred half Shares of £5 each	£17,925
Debenture Loans at 4% per annum	£24,000
"B" Debenture Loans at 5% per annum	£450
	£89,345

7) "Terrier" 0-6-0 tank No. 79 on a westbound Motor train at Dyke Junction Halt. (M. Joly)

On 27 April 1895 the "Brighton Herald" published an article entitled "The Struggles of the Dyke Railway" in which it was stated by the Hon. Ashley Ponsonby at the ordinary meeting on 22 April 1895 that the returns for the half year July to December 1894 showed an increase of about 7,000 in the passenger traffic over the corresponding half year of 1893, bringing the total number carried during the six months to 90,106; this increase being too small to be of any consequence. It was reported that the proportion of the receipts taken by the L.B.S.C.R. was very considerable, Mr Warren, the Secretary, stating that 70 per cent was lost to the Brighton Company as liabilities were gradually paid off. The fate of the Brighton and Dyke Railway Company and its Chairman and directors looked uncertain as financial failure loomed.

On 18 October 1895 a petition was preferred into the High Court of Justice (Chancery Division) for a Receiver to be appointed. The petition was made by Henry Warren, the Secretary of the Company; Thomas Yates, a solicitor; and James Powell, solicitor of the Company. No one appeared for the Brighton and Dyke Railway Company although they were duly served with notice of the application. The Court appointed John F. R. Daniel as Receiver by an Order dated 18 November 1895 — Mr Daniel was Managing Director of the Weston, Clevedon, and Portishead Railway.

The Company was to continue in Receivership until absorption in 1924 into the Southern Railway after spending only 18 of its 47 years of existence since the incorporating Act of 1877 in a state of liquidity. Accounts were not published after 1895 and the only figures available to show the receipts of the line were in 1913 to comply with the Railway Companies (Accounts and Returns) Act, 1911. The state of capital raised by the Company was unchanged since that published by Bradshaw for 1894 but revenue receipts and expenditure for the whole undertaking were published and are shown in Appendix (v).

In accordance with the Grouping of all railway companies in 1923 the Brighton and Dyke Railway Company passed into the complete ownership of the Southern Railway by an Absorption Scheme dated 22 July 1924. From this date the Brighton and Dyke Company was dissolved and all stockholders of the Company were obliged to accept the stock of the Southern Railway Company. The Receiver was discharged and handed over to the Southern Railway all moneys in his possession.

8) Stroudley D-tank No. B627 has run round a "Balloon" in 1927. (J. S. Gray)

CHAPTER THREE

Life of the Railway

(i) The Halts

When the branch was opened there was little serious contemplation of intermediate stations but during the course of the line's history two halts were constructed on the branch itself and another at the junction of the Brighton to Portsmouth line.

The first of these halts was the private Golf Club Halt, opened in 1891, which was 62 chains short of the terminus and on the "up" side of the line. This halt was constructed purely for the benefit of the Brighton and Hove Golf Club, which was opened in October 1887 and one of three in the vicinity at that time. It consisted of a brick platform of substantial length with a nameboard and was about 50 yards from the Club House. There was no shelter or lighting provided. The L.B.S.C.R. Appendix to the Service Time Book of June 1917 gives the following instruction to staff;

"A platform at the Golf Club House is in use for Passengers to join, or leave trains, but the Station Masters at Brighton, Hove, and the Dyke, as well as the guards, must take care that no train, unless it is carrying the train staff, is stopped at this plaform either to take up or set down passengers.

"When trains are carrying the train staff, drivers and guards running from Dyke to Brighton must always keep a good look out for passengers standing on the platform, and arrange to stop thereat to take them up.

"When ordinary trains are employed to work this service on the Dyke railway in place of the Motor Cars, Special Carriages must be locked up by the Conductor before starting, for passengers to and from the Halt, and the driver must always be advised before starting what part of the train is to be stopped alongside the platform at the Halt."

An explanation will be given later in this Chapter concerning "Motor" and "ordinary" trains.

Golf Club Halt never appeared in any timetable and golfers were always obliged to book to the Dyke as no fares or tickets were specifically introduced for their benefit.

On 9 January 1895 an agreement was concluded with the L.B.S.C.R. to install an electric bell in the Club House which would be actuated by the lowering of the starting signal at the Dyke and would ring until the signal was replaced. Thus golfers had sufficient warning to down their drinks at the bar and hurry to the platform to signal the train to stop! The L.B.S.C.R. undertook to install the bell and wire at their expense and also to maintain the system but the Club was obliged to contribute a sum of ten shillings per annum towards the latter. This rental remained unchanged until 1922, when an agreement of 21 June raised it to two pounds.

The Brighton and Hove Golf Club have always kept a most interesting Suggestions Book which contains many references to the

9) Stroudley "D" class B113 waiting to leave the Dyke on a two-coach train in March 1927. (H. C. Casserley)

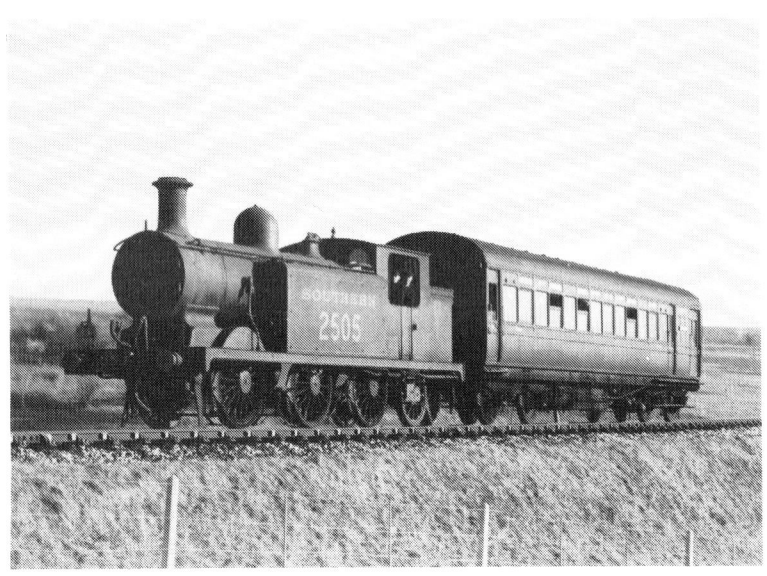

10) E4 No. 2505 ascends the 1 in 40 with a Marsh "Balloon". (Lens of Sutton)

railway. Many suggestions by members of the Club related to the time table; for instance, in October 1896 it was suggested that the Committee of the Club request the L.B.S.C.R. to arrange a Sunday morning train from Brighton at 10.00 am during the winter months. The request is endorsed, "Train provided". On 9 October 1900 no less than 32 signatures accompanied a request to alter the 3.50 pm down train to 4.15 pm in winter. The train service was altered accordingly. One particularly flamboyant entry appears during August 1900 when it was suggested that "a representation be made to the L.B.S.C.R. Company suggesting that some arrangement should be made of the trains from Brighton to the Dyke at 12 and 2.50 during the winter months in the interests of the professional and business members of the Club who are at present practically debarred from using either of these trains, 12 being too early for them to leave their work, and 2.50 too late to permit a round" (of golf) "before dark." Beneath the request is the comment, "On and after 1 September 1900 the present train leaving at 12 noon will leave Brighton at 12.40 and Hove at 12.44."

In 1894 a member suggested that the L.B.S.C.R. erect a shelter on the platform. The Railway Company were duly approached and agreed to build a shelter at a cost to the Club of £100. The Committee decided not to accept the offer but left the matter open to members to raise the money. The suggestion of erecting a shelter between the platform and the Club House was considered but nothing came of this and there is no evidence to suggest that there was ever a shelter at the halt.

In 1904 two signatures in the Suggestions Book appeared against a request that the Steward should give notice in the luncheon room that the bell notifying the departure of the train from the Dyke was ringing. The Steward subsequently received orders to do so. A member who, in 1909, requested the Committee to take steps to remove the difficulty of conveying bicycles from the train to the Club House was not successful in gaining response.

It is interesting to note that the first Secretary of the Club, who was appointed in 1901, was remunerated the sum of £150 per annum plus a Season Ticket from Brighton to the Dyke.

Mr R. M. Gordon-Seymour, a one time user of the halt, remembers that the railway was well used by golfers right up to closure; despite the fact that the motor car was coming into its own, many members of the Brighton and Hove Golf Club remained faithful to their private platform believing the railway to be, in Mr Gordon-Seymour's words, "better, quicker, and cheaper than the motor car."

The second halt to be opened on, or for, the branch was Dyke Junction Halt on 3 September 1905. It was situated on the Brighton to Portsmouth main line and consisted of two platforms of wooden construction on the Brighton side of the Junction Signalbox. Dyke Junction Halt was opened simultaneously with three other halts of similar construction on the main line; Holland Road, Fishergate, and Ham Bridge (now East Worthing). These four halts were to be served by the new "Motor Service" introduced by the L.B.S.C.R. between Brighton and Worthing. The Motor trains were formed of

11) Rowan Halt. (L. Singleton)

12) Golf Club Halt on 12th March 1939 — ten weeks after closure.
(J. S. Gray/A. Bissell)

push-pull carriages propelled by "Terrier" 0-6-0 tank locomotives. Dyke Junction Halt was naturally served by the Dyke trains and, surviving the closure of the line, is still open today as Aldrington, a name taken on 17 June 1932.

The third halt to be opened was Rowan Halt, half a mile from the junction on 12 January 1934. The purpose was to serve the new Aldrington Manor Estate north of the Old Shoreham Road, and it was situated behind Rowan Avenue in Hove. The halt was of wooden construction, the 70ft long platform being on the "up" side of the line; a corrugated iron shelter and iron footbridge were provided. An opening ceremony was performed which was reported in the "Brighton Gazette" the following day. The Mayor of Hove (Councillor V. Hudson, J.P.), formally opened the halt after journeying with his party from Hove in the Sentinel Railbus (to be described later in this Chapter) which was decorated with bunting for the occasion. Music was played over a loudspeaker system as the party arrived and the Mayor enthused, "The manner in which this part of the town has grown is really wonderful. The necessity of the halt has arisen solely out of the enterprise of Messrs. Braybon who have developed the Aldrington Manor Estate. The halt is also a proof of the great foresight of the Southern Railway, whose earnest desire is to cater for the transport needs of the public." The ceremony was broadcast to the Aldrington Manor Estate around which the Mayoral party subsequently toured. Lunch was served at the First Avenue Hotel, Hove. The "Brighton Gazette" interestingly indicated that in 1932 a mere 11,000 passengers were carried on the branch, although this doubled in the following year.

Rowan Halt was to be served by the Motor trains from Brighton, worked by Stroudly D1 0-4-2 tanks, which terminated at the halt at certain times of the day. In 1938 nine trains made Rowan their terminus on weekdays (See Appendix (iii)). This arrangement was excellent for workers travelling home to lunch from Brighton as well as to and from work in the morning and evening. The standard service of Billington E4 0-6-2 tanks and ordinary bogie stock continued to work through to the summit. It is interesting to note that in an effort to sell houses in this ever-developing area, one estate agent invented a bogus "Hangleton Halt", supposedly situated further up the branch!

(ii) Operation

As already stated, in 1905 a push-pull Motor service was introduced on the Brighton to Worthing line. These Motor trains also worked up to the Dyke, the service being operated by D. E. Marsh's first "Balloon" vehicles built at Brighton Carriage Works. These were numbered 1326 and 1327 and were 54ft in length, weighing 23 tons 6 cwt tare, with a seating capacity of 60. The seats were mostly reversible and entrance to these gas-lit "Balloons" was by a door opening inwards for passengers and by a sliding door for the driver. The "Balloons", so called because of their domed roofs, sometimes worked to the Dyke with non-motor trailers when traffic demanded. Interestingly, one of the first two "Balloons" was to work

13) Stroudley 0-4-2 tank "Seaford" at the Dyke with a six-wheeler and two "Balloons".
(Lens of Sutton)

on the very last train of all, as S.R. No. 3829, but stripped of its control gear and modernised with electric lighting. One peculiarity of Marsh's "Balloons" was that they had no hand-brake and were thus to be regarded with some trepidation by the authorities when working the branch on the Motor trains. There is evidence to suggest that Motor working was not perpetuated for very long after the introduction of the "Balloons". The authorities decided to abolish it some time after 1917 and insist on the locomotive leading at all times. Thus the locomotive always had to run round at the terminus and owing to the difficulties in watering at Brighton station a fresh engine had to be attached for each journey. There were never any watering facilities, incidentally, at the Dyke.

The most popular locomotives on the branch were the Billington E4 0-6-2 tanks, with Stroudley D1 0-4-2 tanks probably taking second place. There is evidence that a wide variety of locomotive classes worked on the line at one time or other, the largest tank locomotives being the I1X and I2 4-4-2 classes. Tender locomotives did occasionally wend their way to the summit — these were usually Classes C2, or C2X, 0-6-0s, on ballast trains.

The Dyke branch was operated under the train staff and ticket system when opened. The staff stations were Hove and the Dyke and ticket colour was red. On 6 October 1920 the L.B.S.C.R. changed the system to Webb and Thompson's Electric Train Staff, the staff being exchanged at the junction. There was a telephone circuit which encompassed Dyke Signalbox, Dyke Booking Office, Dyke Junction Signalbox, and Hove Station Master, and the branch had its own telegraphic code — "DY".

The L.B.S.C.R. Appendix to the Service Time Book of June 1917 gives the following regulation;

"No engine must work on the Dyke Railway unless it is fitted with the Westinghouse brake and this must be in thorough working order. The driver must ascertain, by personal inspection, that the taps on the connections between each carriage are open with main pipe, and he must not start with a train if any of the brakes are shut off. The train must not be started from Hove, or from the Dyke station, until the guard has tested the brake by putting it full on, by opening the cock on the rear vehicle; the driver will be held personally responsible that this is done on every occasion before starting the train from either of these stations."

The 1922 Appendix gives the following information;

Signal Box	Weekdays		Sundays	
	Open	Close	Open	Close
Dyke Junction	9.55 am	5.55 pm	9.45 am	12.50 pm
			2.20 pm	5.45 pm
			Closed winter	
Dyke	10.26 am	5.30 pm	10.16 am	5.30 pm
			Closed winter	

At Dyke Junction the Box was switched out when closed, signal lights left burning and main line signals lowered. The Appendix goes on to say that during the times the line was closed the Junction signalmen would be held responsible for seeing that no train was admitted to the branch without proper written or printed instructions. Furthermore, Station Masters and Inspectors were not to allow a train to run on the branch when closed unless the Stations and signalboxes concerned were given previous notice.

In company with many other small branch lines the Dyke railway was closed completely during the First World War from 1 January 1917 until 26 July 1920. Track was left in situ and the closure was purely an economy measure.

In 1921 the branch was used for experimenting and demonstrating the Angus Train Control System. Mr A. R. Angus was an Australian engineer who devised a system of controlling train movements. Before the First World War trials were made in Russia, Sweden, and on the West Somerset Mineral Railway.

On 22 September 1921 tests were carried out in the presence of Colonel Pringle of the Ministry of Transport, the Signal and Telegraph Engineer of the London and South Western Railway, the Electrical Engineer of the Great Central Railway, an adviser to Chinese Government Railways, and others. Mr Angus had obtained permission from the L.B.S.C.R., by agreement dated 18 March 1920, to demonstrate his invention from a point 90ft south of the Old Shoreham Road bridge to the terminus. A temporary water tank was constructed on the "up" side of the line south of the bridge.

The demonstration required the use of two locomotives — these were "Terriers" Nos. 643 and 680 — and involved sending one engine into a section of track occupied by the other. When this occurred steam was automatically shut off and the brakes applied. Each locomotive was fitted with a device which supplied a low voltage alternating current to the track so long as the section was clear. Whenever an obstruction was placed in the section, i.e. another train in this case, the train was brought to a halt even though the driver would not touch the controls. The trials continued for some time and although apparently successful, the system was eventually dismantled.

Mr Angus was obliged to pay the L.B.S.C.R. the sum of £2 per day in weekly instalments for the use of the two locomotives in addition to insuring the Company and himself for £5,000.

The first train to run up to the Dyke every morning was the mixed train which consisted of passenger and goods vehicles with a goods brake van at the rear with a Goods Guard. The outwards goods traffic consisted of coal and coke and cattle food (oil cake and cotton cake) and various small consignments. The inwards goods traffic was mainly baled straw and trussed hay. Parcels traffic received was generally for the three adjacent Golf Clubs, plus the Dyke Hotel and villages of Fulking and Poynings. The delivery of parcels was undertaken by the local coal merchant who collected from the Railway Company the sum of one penny for each package delivered. Evidently the goods traffic was insufficient to justify

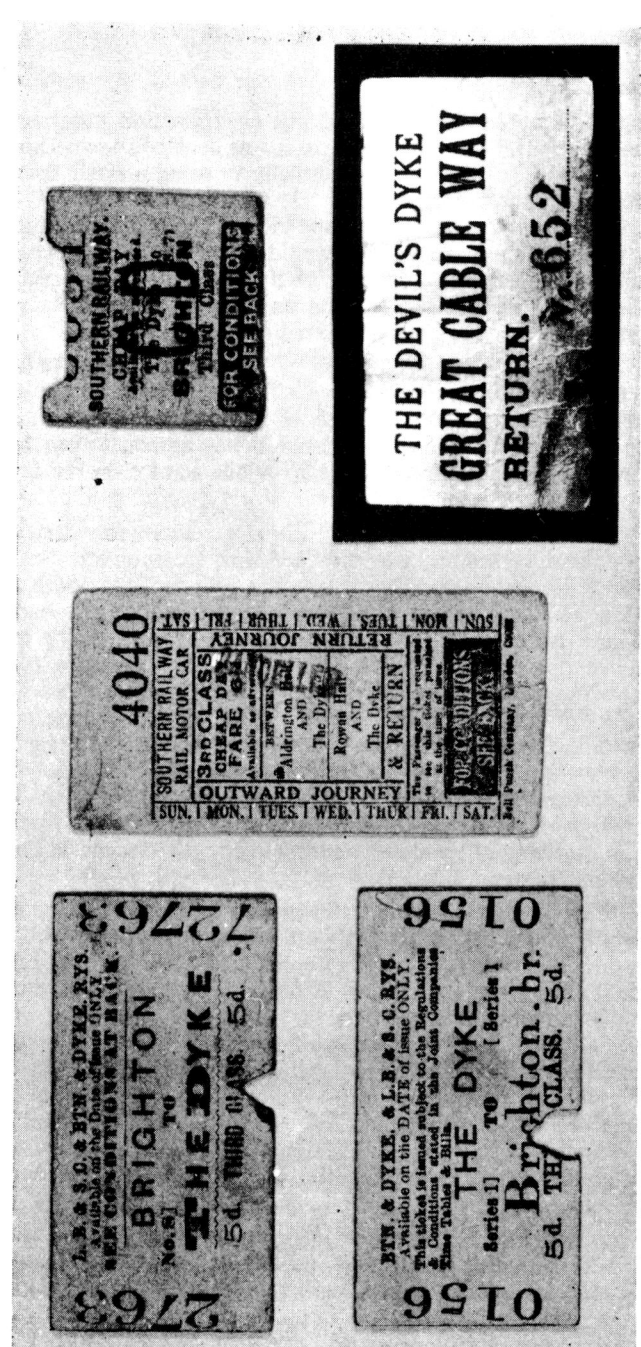

14) A selection of Tickets reproduced full size.

retention of the siding at the terminus and this traffic ceased from 2 January 1933.

(iii) Sentinel Railbus

When the Southern Railway third rail electrification programme was extended beyond the suburban area it was decided to experiment with a steam railbus with a view eventually to using a small fleet to act as feeder services for the new electric line on some of the smaller branches which were to escape electrification. In addition it was felt that maximum economies would be made. The idea of a steam railbus was not new; the first of the modern type in regular service in Britain ran on the London and South Western Railway in 1903 and examples had been conceived as early as 1848.

In 1932 the Sentinel Wagon Works of Shrewsbury, with the help of a steam motor-car designer from California, named Doble, collaborated with Metropolitan Cammell, of Birmingham, to produce a prototype steam railbus. The Southern Railway agreed to purchase the prototype for £2,680 and put it into public service on the Dyke branch.

The railbus, numbered 6 for some obscure reason, was designed to be one-man operated and was provided with an automatic stoking mechanism. The length over bodywork was 48ft 4in, the width 8ft, height 11ft, and two bolster bogies carried the lightweight underframe. The 97hp engine was a two-cylinder compound — the high pressure cylinder being $4\frac{1}{2}$in diameter and the low pressure cylinder $7\frac{1}{2}$in, with a common stroke of 6in. The engine was fitted with Stephenson link motion operated piston valves, all the working parts being enclosed in an oil chamber. The engine was small enough to be slung between the bogie wheels and was arranged horizontally and nose-suspended in the fashion of an electric motor. It was geared to drive only one pair of wheels. Also below the floor was the water tank, holding 240 gallons, and a battery for electric lighting, through a generator.

Above the engine was a compartment in the body which housed the standard road wagon design vertical boiler with a working pressure of 325lbs per sq inch. The boiler was fitted with an automatic feed water regulator which actuated a steam driven water-pump and maintained a constant level of water in the boiler. The automatic stoker was controlled from the same pump through a ratchet mechanism and screw, coal being supplied from the 5 cwt capacity bunker above the level of the boiler which was filled through an upper door. The amount of coal delivered to the firebox and the quantity of water supplied were linked at a fixed ratio and it was this complete automation that enabled the railbus to be driven by one man from either end.

The most novel feature of the prototype was the braking mechanism. The wheels, which had wooden centres for quiet running, were of 30in diameter and had roller bearings within. A strip of copper ran from the tyres to the hubs for track circuiting purposes. All axles were provided with outside brake drums operated by a steam cylinder and rodding. The drums were of the same principle as the road

15) Sentinel railbus outside the soft water tanks in Brighton yard.
(Lens of Sutton)

16) Sentinel railbus at the Dyke in 1933.
(Lens of Sutton/H. C. Casserley)

vehicle with internally expanding shoes with Ferodo linings on an underframe linked assembly. Owing to their exposure to the air the drums had excellent cooling conditions.

The railbus was entered by a centrally situated door on either side. A central vestibule divided the vehicle into two compartments, one seating 24 passengers, the other 20. The semi-bucket type seats all faced towards the centre vestibule and were upholstered in moquette.

There were no standard couplings or buffers at each end but merely "bumper bars".

The weight of the railbus was as follows;

	T	C	Q	T	C	Q
	Left side			Right side		
On first pair of weels	2	2	1	2	8	0
Drivers	2	8	1	2	13	1
On third pair of wheels	1	16	3	1	18	1
On fourth pair of wheels	1	16	0	1	16	0
	8	3	1	8	15	2

The irregularities are attributable to the positioning of the water tank and battery box.

	T	C	Q
On engine bogie	9	11	3
On trailing bogie	7	7	0
	16	18	3

The total weight fully laden was recorded as 20 tons 5 cwt. The above details are reproduced with permission from H. Holcroft's "Locomotive Adventure Vol. II" published by Ian Allan Ltd.

The bus was completed by Sentinel in January 1933 and was sent to Metropolitan Cammell in Birmingham to have the body fitted. Before acceptance by the S.R., Sentinel agreed to make alterations to the brakes, which were not considered powerful enough. The railbus was delivered from Birmingham to Brighton on Sunday 19 March 1933. During the journey speeds of up to 60 m.p.h. were attained. Two days later, after trips from Brighton up to Steyning and back for the benefit of drivers, two trial runs were made up to the Dyke. The results are tabulated in Appendix (iv).

On 23 March four more test runs were made. On the first run the railbus came to a stand on the 1 in 40 gradient having lost pressure in the boiler. However, it was proved that this was due to the sticky nature of the mixture of Chislet and hard coal in use, which clogged the grate in the mechanical stoker. During the other ascents made that day boiler pressure was maintained at 290lb per sq. inch or above and full regulator used with cut-offs between 65 and 70 per cent. (These figures must be roughly halved for comparison with simple expansion).

The brakes proved capable of controlling the descents, even when on one occasion the railbus was overloaded with standing passengers.

The following day the railbus was run over the Brighton to Horsham line as far as Southwater and a maximum speed of 66 m.p.h. was attained.

Four more runs were made to the Dyke on 28 March when the $3\frac{1}{2}$ miles of 1 in 40 was climbed in 8-$8\frac{1}{2}$ minutes. The trials then ceased for minor alteration and additions to be made. Among these were the provision of a screen to protect the driver from the heat of the boiler, speedometers, bell communication between driver and guard, and sand pipe guards to prevent the flow being blown by the wind. The horn was made louder and the passengers seats raised. A proposal to make a sliding door in the roof above the boiler to assist ventilation was deferred. Five more trials were carried out on 11th April after which the brake, still thought to be sluggish, was tested but passed as fit.

The railbus finally entered public service on 1 May 1933 resplendent with a gilt-lettered roofboard "Brighton and The Dyke". It was destined always to work to the Dyke on a "one engine in steam" principle with the boiler end leading. The railbus made several more visits to Brighton works for minor adjustments, one of the problems being track circuit failures owing to poor conductivity of the tyres which had no brake blocks to keep them clean. This was solved by periodic wheel washing. The most serious problem which arose was the brakes and Sentinel eventually fitted a larger diameter set of drums.

Mr A. C. Perryman, who was at Brighton Works at the time, has told me how the railbus was supplied with a gear ratio unsuited for the steep gradient. The S.R. had requested this because their prime concern was possible delay to the new electric service between Brighton and the junction at Aldrington Halt, which could have occurred had they opted for a gear ratio for lower speed. Mr Perryman went on to say that as a result drivers often had to stop on the ascent for a "blow-up". He said that the descent was a nightmare as the brakes were proving inadequate and on more than one occasion when they were overheated the railbus ran out of control on the 1 in 40 and was unable to be pulled up until Hove.

Despite these problems the railbus proved to be extremely popular with the public, especially when Rowan Halt was opened on 12 January 1934 and quick access to Hove and Brighton was available. This popularity was to become a serious shortcoming as the bus could not handle the traffic. The attachment of a trailer coach was physically impossible (it would have been doubtful if the summit could have been reached, and the descent would have been dangerous had this been possible) and on many occasions an E4 0-6-2 tank with two coaches had to be substituted, principally at weekends.

As a result of the experience gained from the Dyke railbus, Sentinel improved their design and were asked by the S.R. to quote for five more railbuses, principally for the Staines, Ascot, Camberley, Aldershot lines, the Westerham branch, and the Three Bridges to Horsham line. The price was higher than the S.R. expected and it proved impossible to raise the seating capacity; the decision was taken not to proceed.

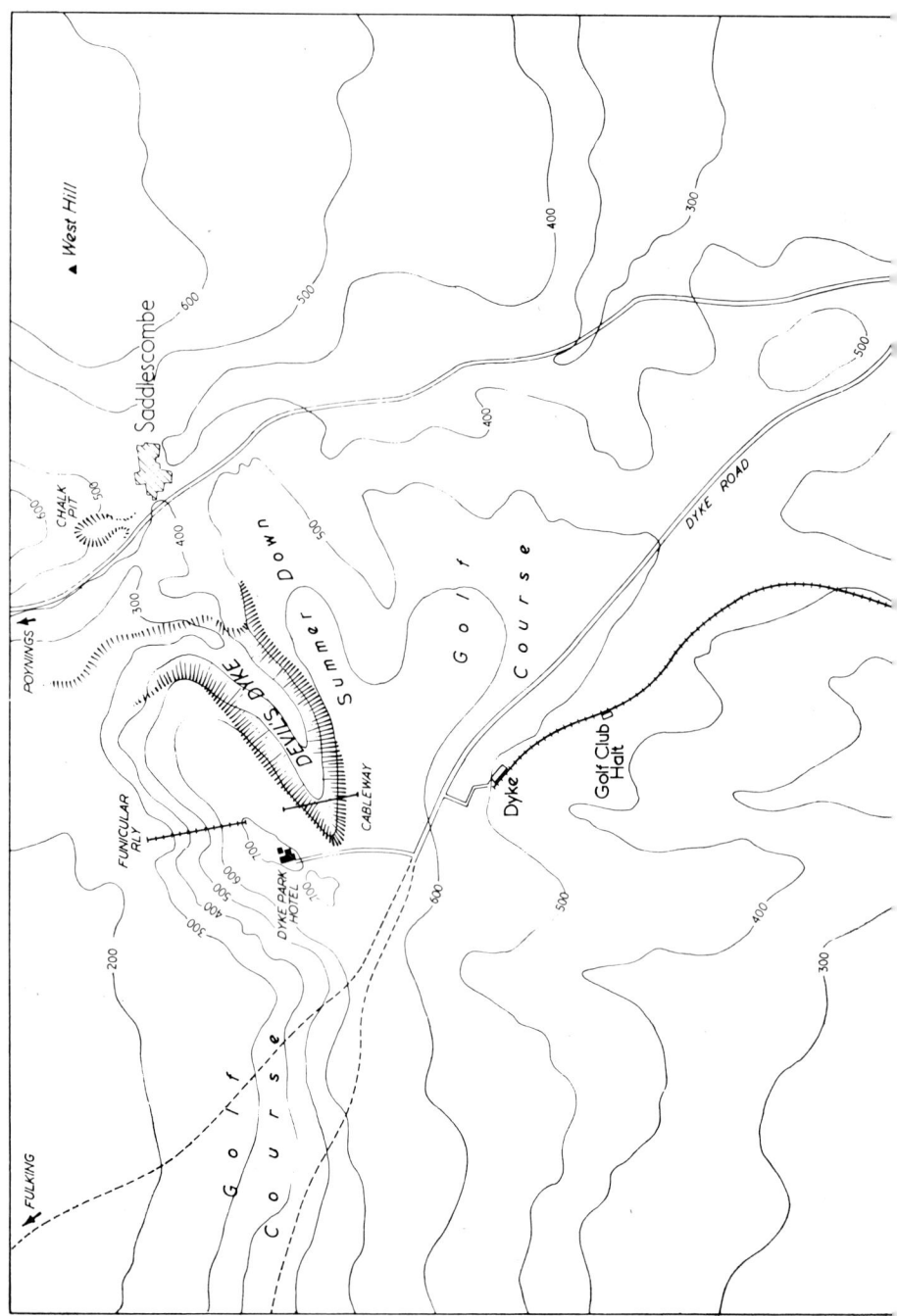

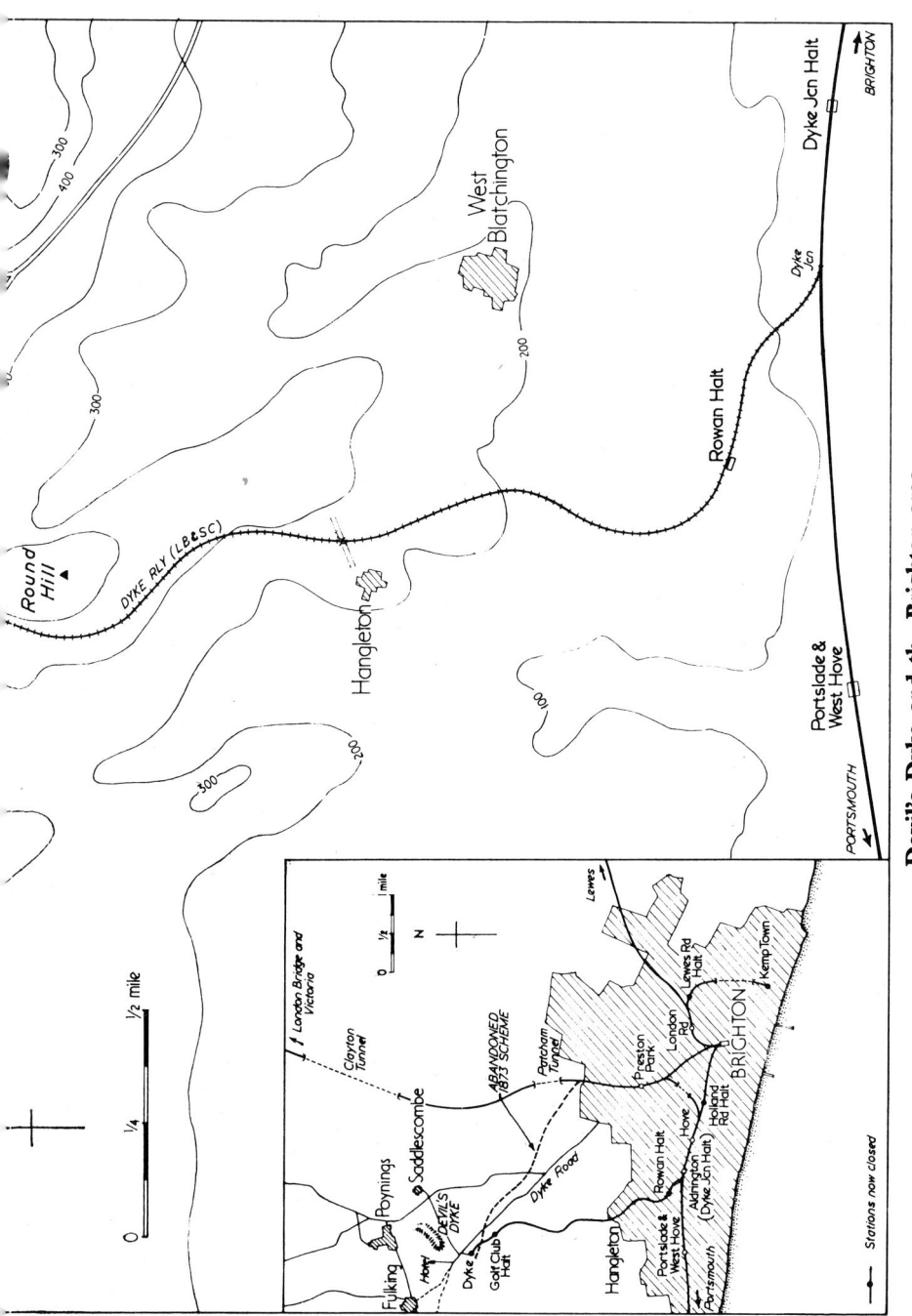

Devil's Dyke and the Brighton area

17) The Railbus seen at The Dyke in 1934. (L. Singleton)

18) Hangleton Road Bridge in 1935. After closure the road was filled in to rail level during the 1940s. (J. S. Gray)

The railbus was to continue in service on the Dyke branch until 1 May 1935 when it suffered a fractured bogie bolster. This was repaired but owing to the difficulties in handling the number of passengers the railbus was never to return to service on the line again. It was eventually sent to work the Westerham branch and the E4 0-6-2 tanks were reinstated on the Dyke line on a permanent basis. The railbus continued in service until 22 April 1937 when it suffered a boiler failure and was stored at Tonbridge until June 1938 when it was towed to Ashford Works. In September 1940 the railbus was stripped of all fittings and saw life as a mess room for the Home Guard and firewatchers. Official withdrawal took place in January 1942, but it was not broken up at Ashford until the Autumn of 1946. The Dyke railbus was the last to be built for railways in Great Britain.

(iv) **Reminiscences**

Mr L. Budd, of Littlehampton, worked at the Dyke in the Summer of 1928 and from February 1929 until October 1930. "I had a wonderful time up there but the winters were bloody awful!" he recalls. Mr Budd was the only man on duty, his duties encompassing porter, signalman, booking clerk, and shunter, and his shift was 9.55 am to 5.55 pm. He always travelled to work at the Dyke on the first train, joining at Hove. If there was a heavy E4 tank on the first service of the day and it was a wet morning the train would frequently slip to a standstill on the 1 in 40 gradient after passing under the Old Shoreham Road. Mr Budd, together with the driver and fireman would climb down and sprinkle sand and cinders for some distance on the rails in front of the train after which the driver would have another run. "The wheels would be spinning but the train would sometimes slip backwards," recalls Mr Budd. If the locomotive could still not master the wet rails the train would set back to Hove Corporation Sidings after depositing the passengers at the Junction Halt, the locomotive would run round, and the train make its way ignominiously back to Brighton. The passengers together with Mr Budd would join the next service to the Dyke which, hopefully, would be powered by a smaller tank with larger wheel diameter and greater adhesion and successfully reach the summit.

Mr Budd travelled home on the last train from the Dyke every day. The platform starter was left in the "on" position and the driver instructed to pass the signal at danger. The home signal, however, was always pulled off ready for the first train in the morning. The Electric Train Staff was locked in a cabinet at Dyke Junction Signalbox and not in the machine. Unless this was done the first train would not be able to gain the branch until the button was depressed in Dyke Signalbox to give "line clear" and release the Staff from the machine at the junction.

On one occasion the Staff fell off the bracket on the locomotive on the descent from the Dyke. When the train arrived at the junction the driver reported the loss whereupon the signalman permitted the train to proceed. A man from Hove and a telegraph lineman had to walk the entire length of the branch to confirm the line was clear before another train was allowed to run. The lineman had to remove a Staff from the machine to equalise the number before the junction signalman could release his Staff. The lost Staff was eventually found at the foot of an embankment by a ganger.

Life at the Dyke was certainly lonely for Mr Budd — "Sometimes in the winter the only people I'd see all day would be the drivers and firemen of the locomotives. There would not be a single passenger on the trains!" Bank Holidays were different, however, for Mr Budd would deal with several thousand passengers in a single day and have a booking clerk, ticket collector, shunter, and porter to assist him in his duties.

On one occasion he was in the process of uncoupling a Class 12 locomotive after the arrival of a train when he nearly came to grief. "I nearly had my chips with No. 15," he says. "The driver moved off before I'd finished, with me hanging on the coupling. He got quite a shock when he looked round and saw the train still with him."

Mrs F. Pettit, of Hassocks, can remember travelling on the train when it was so overladen, and travelling so slowly on the ascent, that she and her fellow passengers used to get out, pick blackberries, and catch it up again.

One Good Friday, the train was travelling so slowly that the guard, after telling passengers riding in the brake van not to touch the brakes, climbed down and walked by the side of the train picking wild flowers for them.

Another occasion when the train came to a complete stand was when the well known Rev. Dick Sheppard gave an open-air address at the Dyke. The train was very heavily laden and while the locomotive was standing at Rowan Halt building up steam on the 1 in 40 many passengers decided to climb down and complete the journey across the fields by foot. This lightened the train considerably and when the driver coaxed his mount into action again he kept going and those who alighted were unable to get on again.

Once when the mixed train was climbing to the Dyke a Shunter named Peter Thornton took his shot-gun with him and bowled over a nice fat hare from the train as the summit was approached.

A splendid tale concerning the Electric Train Staff can be told. The last train of the day was travelling down from the Dyke on an occasion when a relief signalman was on duty at Dyke Junction. He was probably unfamiliar with the procedure of locking the Staff in a cabinet and not in the machine, so that the Dyke signalman could travel up on the first train next day. When the Staff was given up the relief signalman put it in the machine by mistake. Realising what he had done the wretched man telephoned Hove ticket office. The learner clerk who answered the 'phone had no idea what to do. He asked the clerk, who was busy; then he asked the Foreman — a redfaced individual with large boots — who was furious. The 5.08 pm London Bridge to Bognor was due, and with it a passenger who dispensed largesse in the form of 1/- per day to the porter — always the Foreman — who carried his bag to the carriage waiting to take him home. On this awful day, through having to attend to the woes of some idiot relief signalman at Dyke Junction "who has put the Staff in the instrument and he can't get it OUT!!!" the Foreman missed his shilling. He danced with rage, heavy booted, on the wooden floor of the ticket office.

One morning when the first train was returning to Brighton it met a large horse on the line. Whistling and the blowing of cylinder drain cocks made no impression on the beast. The fireman was sent forward to remove the animal but as he advanced shouting and waving his arms, the horse looked coolly at him. Then it began to walk purposefully towards the advancing fireman, who, not being a country lad, was overwhelmed by the size of the beast. After a final yell, it was the fireman who bolted — for the engine! The horse turned round and walked off down the line, followed at a respectful distance by the train.

On many occasions the drivers of the Dyke trains had to put out, on the way back, the lineside fires their locomotives had started on the way up. During at least one winter a train was unable to reach the terminus owing to a snow drift which had to be shovelled through.

Mr A. Geere, of Brighton, remembers working the last train from the Dyke one night when the Train Staff was accidentally left on the platform at the terminus. Its absence was not realised until the train had all but reached Dyke Junction and there was nothing for it but to go back to the summit to collect the Staff.

Another driver on the Dyke railway was Mr F. Gambling, of Brighton, who recalls that the Billington E4 0-6-2 tanks were the locomotives best suited to the line. Mr Gambling remembers that double-heading was used on some heavily loaded services but an E4 with four bogies was the norm during a busy period. He also recalls taking a ballast train up to the Dyke with a C2 0-6-0. In addition to the brake van at the rear of the train, another was included half way just in case the locomotive stalled and splitting the load became necessary. On this occasion, however, the summit was reached. He also recalls that after dark, golfers wishing to join the last train from the Dyke would strike matches to signal to the driver to stop the train at the unlit Golf Club Halt!

(v) Closure

The demise of the Dyke railway came on 31 December 1938. The reason was quite simple; the internal combustion engine was coming into its own by the 1930s and visitors were able to make their way to the Hotel by omnibus without a wearying 200ft climb by foot from Dyke station. Traffic had been falling steadily for years and whilst the trains were filled to capacity at Bank Holidays the winter months unhappily saw too few people to make the railway economically viable. The porter-signalman then at the Dyke, John Weller, was to be found another job at Hove.

The last train from Brighton to the Dyke was the 5.07 pm returning at 5.37 pm. The train was formed of one of the ex-L.B.S.C.R. "Balloons", soon to be broken up, and a three coach ex-South Eastern and Chatham Railway set, hauled by E4 0-6-0 No. 2505.

A reporter from the "Brighton Gazette" was a passenger on the last train and his racy account gives a vivid description of a scene to become all too familiar in later years;

LAST JOURNEY OF THE DYKE "EXPRESS"
CROWD OF 350 BESEIGE PLATFORM

"The Devil's Dyke people want a Square Deal — but the Southern Railway wants one too, so the outcome of decreasing traffic on the Brighton-Dyke Railway is their decision to close down the line after trains have been puffing their way into the South Downs for 51 years.

"And the Dyke folk say it is the Railway's fault. In the summer time there is an evening train to and from the Dyke, but in winter time this is dispensed with, as the last train from Brighton is then the 5.07 the Dyke contingent has to depend on the bus service.

"So on Saturday the 5.07 made history. New Year's Eve and the day chosen to close the Dyke line — $5\frac{1}{2}$ miles of single track, winding up through Aldrington, Rowan, and the Brighton and Hove Golf Course. Normally, the 5.07 is a single coach, 3rd class, with one compartment for smokers, and the other for non-smokers . . . but on occasions like this there are always those souvenir fiends who want to be at the death. A special train was put into service.

Platform beseiged

"And while I was talking to Mr F. T. Roach, Brighton's Station Master, complete in his shining topper, and Mr Bob Pitt, that well known Brighton licensee, who travelled in the first Dyke train in 1887, the platform was beseiged.

"Apart from the opening day just over half a century ago, I doubt whether the Dyke 'Express' has ever been so crowded.

"Close on 350 people wanted to buy the last ticket, they came armed with paper hats and coloured streamers — the relics of Christmas — and there were musicians and tin-whistle, a piano accordian, and a fiddle.

"Awaiting the 5.07 at the Dyke was Porter Weller — John Charles Weller, porter signalman, coupler, ticket collector, booking clerk, and 'Stationmaster' at his lonely outpost on the South Downs.

"Never in his 20 years with the Railway Company had he had a day like Saturday, and few porters in their time have the privilege of closing down a railway line, or even a wayside halt. But this duty fell to John Weller on Saturday.

Whistles and fog signals

"As we steamed out from Brighton Station a volley of fog signals, and piercing shrieking engine whistles from the repair sheds, heralded the start of eleven miles of history — to the Dyke and back nearly 400 of us sang to the music of the band in the saloon coach. People in houses along the Dyke line drew back their blinds and waved, crowds gathered on each platform and level crossing to cheer the 'Express' on its way, and all along our route we met volley after volley of fog signals.

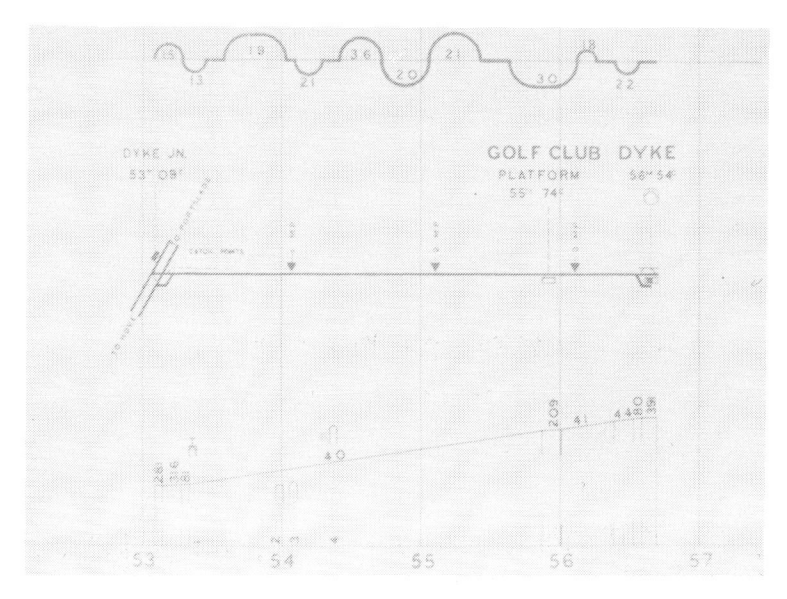

19) Gradient profile. (Courtesy P. Hay)

20) The last run; 31st December 1938.

"And so on to the Dyke and non stop through the Golf Club 'station'.

"Porter Weller treated the 5.07 just like any other train he has welcomed at the Dyke. He took the 'staff' from the engine driver, shifted the points, uncoupled the engine and superintended shunting the engine to the other end of the train. He looked after the signal-box, clipped tickets, and went back to the booking office to sell me the last Dyke-Brighton ticket.

"Actually I bought the last ticket five times and nearly missed the train.

"Each time other souvenir hunters wanted a ticket I had to retail the one I had already bought.

"And when 'station master' Weller had set his signals for the last time he was serenaded along the platform by our voluntary band. In the flickering light of oil lamps we sang Auld Lang Syne, wore paper hats, and caught the 'flu.

"We were due out at 5.37 and in spite of ceremonies like this some attention has to be paid to schedules, and all that sort of thing. Top-hatted Mr Roach sat back in his reserved 1st class carriage, the guard watched good-naturedly, and the engine driver let off steam.

"The return trip was started at 5.47 — just 10 minutes late, but excusable in such circumstances as these and the Southern Railway provided something like 50 more fog signals to let the Dyke people hear their last train leaving for Brighton.

"And Mr Roach had brought with him special destination boards for this last journey.

'JOURNEY'S END 1887-1938' they read.

Square deals

"I have spoken to some of the Dyke people who are affected by this change.

"Not far away, in a cottage overlooking the station, Mrs Saunders was thinking of railways and 'square deals'.

"Every morning for 7 years she has gone into Brighton by train — for years it cost her 1s 4d to fetch her bread, meat, and groceries each day.

" 'I deal in stores in Brighton, but they only deliver once a fortnight so I find it essential to go shopping at Brighton every day', she told me. Mrs Saunders is well known to day trippers to the Dyke, for she serves tea to weary walkers — and the grocery side of the question is going to be a worrying one now that the train service had been done away with.

" 'During the recent snowfall the trains were invaluable, for the buses were not running and without the trains I should have been completely marooned', she went on.

Picked up two golfers

"The 5.37 usually 'flashes' through the Golf Club 'station' but on Saturday it was different — we stopped to pick up a couple of golfers, with plus fours and golf bags, making the journey for the last time.

"The return trip was rowdier than the outward journey. The crowd at the halts had grown and nearly every blind was drawn in the houses along our route.

"The Golf Club 'station', grass covered and deserted, does not see many passengers, and trains to and from Brighton pass non-stop unless a likely passenger is sighted.

"Most of the members of the Brighton and Hove Golf Club go to the club-house by car nowadays — except in snowy weather, and the 11.07 from Brighton drops them a stone's throw away from the 'nineteenth'.

"Lieutenant-Colonel P. J. Reeves, Secretary of the Club, told me that the closing of the railway affects the Brighton and Hove Golf Club. 'In a small way it is a serious loss to us', he said. 'In the days before cars were popular, all our members used to come by train, and they were landed almost at the club-house door, and even now in times of snow and ice the railway is useful if cars and buses are unable to get through', he said.

They will miss it most

"For 26 years, Mr Walker Clifford, of Fulking Grange, had depended on the Dyke Railway for his visits to Brighton and Hove. He lives right out on the Downs — 20 minutes walk from the station, but without a road to walk on. 'My family will miss the Dyke trains more than anybody for we have used it for the last 26 years several times a week', he told me. Mr Clifford has a young daughter who goes to work in Brighton every day . . . she will have to go by car now. 'At one time people from the Dyke had to pay 1s 4d return to Brighton, while people coming out from Brighton could have cheap tickets at $8\frac{1}{2}$d in each direction', said Mr Clifford.

"Farmer Williams, of Dyke Farm, indignantly waving his stick and shouting to me to 'get off' mistook me for one of the hundreds of hikers who walk over his farm and leave his gates wide open in the course of each year. 'I've had all my feeding stuffs sent up by train, but now it has to come by lorry, and I don't have to use the trains to get from here to Brighton.'

"I thought of these people at the Dyke as the 5.37 drew in at Brighton. There were more detonators, engine whistle shrieking, and music on the arrival platform. Even the driver and stoker donned paper hats. For eightpence ha'penny return (cheap day) it was a 'value-for-money' trip, with the comfort of a 1st class carriage thrown in gratis by Mr Roach.

"A page in history for the railway, but a black day for the Dyke people."

Indeed it was. There were to be more passenger trains on the branch that day — three more Motors ran to Rowan Halt. The very last one of all was the 8.00 pm from Brighton and 8.31 pm from Rowan hauled by D1 0-4-2 No. 2699.

CHAPTER FOUR

The Aerial Cableway

Although the standard gauge line from Brighton was opened in 1887 the first move to construct a transport novelty at the Dyke was in 1893 when a civil engineer named William Brewer, "hailing from the land of cuteness and dollars" as the "Brighton Gazette" put it, set about designing a scheme which was to prove only partly successful. Mr Brewer's proposals were of a threefold character;

1. A light cable tramway from the existing standard gauge station to the Dyke Estate; this never materialised.
2. An aerial flight across the ravine.
3. A contrivance by which passengers could be carried backwards and forwards at the steep declivity of the Punch Bowl.

The third of the alternatives was eventuaally constructed in 1897 as the Steep Grade Railway on the north side on Dyke Hill. The "Brighton Gazette" on 16 September 1893 described the proposals thus;

> "The aerial flight across the Dyke proper will be the longest in the world, and will certainly prove a triumph of engineering skill. A cable will be anchored on either side of the Dyke, which will carry a car, and being made to rise by means of rapidly revolving fans, will relieve the trolly of a great proportion of its weight. Then the tramway to the Punch Bowl will convey passengers either to the top or base in the space of three minutes, while the 'Bowl' itself will be prettily laid out as tea gardens, and other attractions provided. The whole scheme has been carefully thought out, and the fact that Mr Brewer has had the assistance of Mr Scott-Russell and Mr Lothian is a sufficient guarantee that the best scientific knowledge has been brought to bear upon it, and that all that human skill can do has been done to ensure the safety of the passengers, several patents being involved. As a commercial speculation the scheme cannot fail to be of the most remunerative character.
>
> "This is no wild or visionary or chimerical undertaking. In the first place, the expenses are comparatively nil, inasmuch as by the manner in which the tramway will be constructed one car will haul the other; there will be no fuel to provide, or expensive machinery to maintain, and the only item will be electricity, which will be the motive power. At Scarborough the lift tramway pays 20 per cent dividend, and the Hastings Company recently declared a dividend of 12 per cent. Then it must be remembered that these are constructed on a much more expensive basis and that they are entirely without novelty. So successful have been the lifts at Folkestone that another is about to be erected. In this instance there will be utility, novelty and exhilarating pleasure combined in one of the most popular recreative resorts in the kingdom.
>
> "Over a million people have visited the Dyke this season, and if only one fourth of this number patronised the tramway, the

aerial flight or the dip into the Punch Bowl, it would suffice to pay the cost of initial construction. That the public appreciate this kind of sensational amusement is proved by the manner in which they patronise the switch-back railways, the toboggan slides and the water 'chute' at the Earl's Court Exhibition, and we confidently predict that the existence of the tramway in question will be the means of attracting even a much larger number to the Dyke than have hitherto gone to that historic spot."

How convincing this account may have been one cannot judge but the only one of Mr Brewer's three schemes to materialise initially was the aerial flight across the ravine, and even that was not operated in the extraordinary manner described, but was, nevertheless, the first of its type ever built.

The aerial cableway was envisaged to play an important part in revolutionising the system of spanning distances over mountainous gorges and rivers and effecting a saving in cost. Mr Brewer, well known as an inventor, had spent some time in the Civil Service in India, where he had first conceived the idea of spanning chasms. In this country he managed to secure patent rights in improvements for devices in aerial navigation; new elevator means and railway and safety grip devices; and improvements in suspension cable tracks for overhead purposes or railway stations. The Devil's Dyke was the first place where Mr Brewer had obtained a concession to put some of these patents to the test and if successful he planned to extend the principle to Cornish mines, Midland factories and pits.

Towards the end of 1893 the promoters, in the form of the Telpher Cable and Cliff Railway Syndicate, Limited, held a number of meetings at Markwell's Hotel, Brighton, which Mr Brewer attended. At these meetings the scheme was fully explained with the help of a detailed drawing and working model.

With Mr Hubbard's backing the cableway was constructed in 1894 at a cost of about £5,000 by the Cable Tramways Construction and Conversion Company Limited; a Company formed in 1883 with a Capital of £200,000, and having as its aims the construction and maintenance of tramways in the United Kingdom.

The installation consisted of 1,200ft of cableway stretched across the ravine. The track cables were suspended from a catenary cable by a series of cast metal supports, having two arms extended outwards and joined to the catenary cable by a vertical rod. The track wheels supporting the cars passed over these anchors, and they were adjusted so as to preclude all possibility of their running off the tracks. One set of wheels controlled the opposite set. The cars were moved by an endless cable worked by a Crossley's patent oil engine adjacent to the north station and not by electricity, as envisaged in the original proposals. One particularly novel feature was the continuity of the line which passed through supports at stated intervals. In other contemporary systems the line would be confined to two given points, necessitating the unslinging and restarting of the cars. There were two cagework cars in use, each seating four passengers and the time taken to cross from one side to the other was about

21) The aerial cableway, looking towards the north station.
(J. S. Gray)

2 minutes 15 seconds. There were small stations on either side of the ravine approximately 1,100ft apart. The height of the cableway from the base of the chasm was 230ft and the clear span between the two huge iron columns supporting the catenary, and embedded in solid masonry, was 650ft. The contractors were Messrs Heenan and Froud, engineers, of Manchester and Birmingham, and the steel wire cables were made by Messrs D. H. and G. Haggie, of Sunderland. The cable rails were less thick than the catenary cable and even if one of the cables parted the stability of the cars would not have been affected, the support provided by the duplication of cables ensuring the cars being maintained in an upright position. The fare charged for the journey was 6d in each direction.

It was unfortunate that construction work was not completed in time for the summer season of 1894, but the cableway was ready for its opening ceremony on 13 October of that year.

A large number of influential municipal and professional luminaries were present at the ceremony, many having travelled in reserved saloon carriages on the 10 am train from London and the 12 o'clock train from Brighton to the Dyke. When everyone was gathered at the north side of the ravine the official inaugural car was despatched carrying the Mayor and Mayoress of Brighton, Mr and Mrs W. Botting, Mr William T. Spink (Chairman of the operating syndicate), and the inventor, Mr Brewer. The car returned amid loud applause and the Mayor formally declared the cableway open laughingly remarking that the Mayoress had considered the graceful and gliding motion as "heavenly". A daughter of one of the

48

22) The cableway, showing the cagework car. (J. S. Gray)

directors, Miss Walter, presented the Mayoress with a bouquet of arum lilies and Japanese chrysanthemums to renewed applause, after which the party adjourned to the Pavilion of the Dyke Estate, suitably decorated with bunting for the occasion. Luncheon was provided by Mr Hubbard, and the Hove Band played a selection of music outside in the fine weather.

After dinner, a somewhat lengthy list of toasts was proposed. Mr Brewer gave the health of the Mayor and Mayoress, and the Mayor, in reply, thanked and congratulated the directors and Mr Brewer. He went on to relate the legend of the "Great Enemy of Mankind" and generally extol the virtues of the Dyke as one of the healthiest places in the whole country. A solicitor, Mr W. C. Croome, proposed the health of the inventor and talked of Mr Brewer's fine character; "Few were aware of the obstacles that had to be surmounted; the getting over the indifference of many, the positive opposition of a few, and, what was most trying, the lukewarm sympathy of others who tapped their foreheads and talked of castles in the air. Mr Brewer had, however, in a literal sense, realised his castle in the air; but he had only been able to do this through the uninterrupted kindness of friends who stood with him throughout the whole of this trying period." Mr Brewer returned thanks after loud applause, and Mr N. Scott-Russell remarked that the one fault in the working was that it was too smooth and that people in their pleasures were not perfectly happy unless they had been turned upside down — Laughter ensued.

More speeches and toasts followed and the company then returned to the cableway station and spent a while journeying over the ravine, the two cars being kept running as fast as possible.

And so the cableway was finally opened despite pessimism from many — indeed some still said it was desecration of a beauty spot — and the directors looked forward to a long and profitable future.

23) The cableway looking east with "Dennett's Corner" restaurant in the foreground. (J. S. Gray)

The "Devil's Dyke Times" assured the user of the "wonderful aerial railway" that the flight across the ravine could be achieved in perfect safety and that "the delight of a trip on this railway can only be experienced, it is too delicious to be described."

Within a few weeks of opening the sensational feeling experienced by the hundreds who had made the journey apparently exhausted its power on one member of the staff engaged on the cableway who actually crossed the wire cables on his hands and knees, a performance requiring iron nerves. This particular individual could frequently be seen scrambling from the car and with the agility of a monkey would traverse the unsubstantial passage-way in a manner to make an observer's hair stand on end! A reporter in the "Hove Gazette", incidentally, was moved to comment at the turn of the century about the view from the cableway — "Rouen Cathedral is not in it!"

Although the aerial cableway had a good start there is evidence that traffic steadily declined in the early years of the new century; indeed, Mr Hubbard suffered financial difficulties and he was eventually to emigrate to Toronto in 1907. Without the promotion of Mr Hubbard the cableway's future was uncertain and it eventually ceased to operate around 1909 although there is no evidence to suggest the exact date. The remains were used as target practice by troops during the First World War when 50lb Cooper bombs were detonated — thus ended the short reign of what can truly be described as the forerunner of the modern mono-rail system.

CHAPTER FIVE

The Steep Grade Railway

The other transport venture provided by Mr Hubbard was the Steep Grade railway. This more ambitious project materialised in 1897 and was a double track narrow gauge funicular (one car ascending as the other descended) on the northern slope of Dyke Hill, known as the Shepherd's Steps, to the picturesque village of Poynings. The cableway had been constructed primarily as a novelty, but the Steep Grade, apart from being a genuine piece of engineering, was to give visitors from Brighton the opportunity to descend on foot to Poynings for dainty Sussex Teas provided by many cottages during the season and returning to the standard gauge station via the Steep Grade and the cableway. Thus there was to be a through route over the South Downs.

There was a frequent service of three-horse-brakes from Brighton to the Dyke during the summer, which usually allowed $\frac{3}{4}$ hour to an hour before the return journey and many visitors, having walked down to Poynings, would find that the only chance to catch their particular vehicle would be to use the Steep Grade.

It was hoped that the Steep Grade would be able to supply the Hotel with farm produce direct from local sources although supplies were also carried up the standard gauge line from Brighton. In addition, farm produce would be carried through to the coast. Mr Hubbard also envisaged that the line would open up his domain to the landward side of the South Downs.

It was estimated that 275,000 passengers would be carried annually on the line. This was roughly the anticipated traffic on the standard gauge line.

With these thoughts in mind Mr Hubbard granted a lease on the land required for the railway to the Pyramidical Syndicate Ltd. of London at a ground rent of £100 per annum, the line to be owned and operated as the Brighton Dyke Steep Grade Railway Ltd.

By an agreement dated 31 December 1896 the Brighton Dyke Steep Railway Ltd. was to pay £9,000 to the Pyramidical Syndicate Ltd. in consideration for the construction of the railway. The agreement stated that £7,000 was to be paid in cash on signing the agreement and within three months 200 debenture bonds of £10 each were to be allotted. The Pyramidical Syndicate Ltd. had the option of subscribing for 2,000 shares at par. The common seal of the Brighton Dyke Steep Grade Railway Ltd. was affixed bearing the motto "vide et crede" ("see and believe").

In the meantime the Company received its Certificate of Incorporation on 9 December 1896. The Memorandum of Association stated the objects of the Company as follows; "to erect at the Dyke, Brighton, or elsewhere, a Steep Grade Railway, or any other Railway or Railways, for use or amusement." The Capital was £10,000 divided into 10,000 shares of £1 each; from this sum £9,000 had to be raised for the construction by the subsequent agreement with the Pyramidical Syndicate Ltd.

The first directors of the Company were;
Major-General Arthur Taylor Penny
Hon. F. Byng
W. D. Pitt, Esq.
Frank Farrant, Esq.

The quorum of directors was two and the qualification other than the first directors was £100 shares each. The directors were remunerated for their services the sum of £2.2.0 per meeting attended. A notice of the situation of the Registered Office of the Company was given on 25 February 1897 by the Secretary, F. Darlington, as 28a Basinghall Street, London, E.C.

The line was to be constructed by Messrs Courtney and Birkett, a yacht building firm of nearby Southwick, who were contractors for the permanent way and hauling gear, and directly responsible to the Pyramidical Syndicate Ltd. To engineer the line, Mr Hubbard had the assistance of Charles O. Blaber, A.M.InstC.E., of Brighton, who was also engineer to the Brighton and Dyke Railway Company.

In anticipation of the formation of an operating comany, the Pyramidical Syndicate Ltd. had drawn up a Specification with Mr Blaber for the contractor as early as April 1896. The following extracts from the Specification are of interest;

"The roadway" (i.e. railway) "is to be formed by removing the surface mould. The embankment to be raised in layers of 6 inches in depth and well rammed and proper allowance for subsidence so that the banks, when handed over at the expiration of the six months maintenance undertaken by the Contractor, may remain."

"The permanent fence to be made on each side of the railway shall be iron continuous. The fence is to be fixed with an inclination outwards from the railway."

The rails provided "shall be subject to a test of a section 6 feet long on bearings 3 feet apart with a weight of 10 cwt falling 10 feet causing a deflection of not more than 4 inches."

"The piles to be pitch pine timber of the best quality perfectly sound and free from stakes, sap, bolt holes, decay or any defects whatever."

The double-track 3ft gauge lines consisted of 35lb per yard Vignoles rails which were laid on 7in x 4in longitudinal sleepers, tied by cross transomes and anchored to piles (6in x 6in x 7ft) driven into the chalk hill in sets of four, at intervals of 30ft, except at embankments where they were 9in x 9in and at intervals of 15ft. The rails were flanged and ballast was maintained between the sleepers. There were three gradients; the lower section being 1 in 2.9; the middle and steepest section 1 in 1.5; and the uppermost section 1 in 1.8. The vertical curves between the gradients were of aproximately 1,000ft radius. By these gradients the 840ft long line rose 395ft.

It was decided to house the driving machinery at the top of the slope. To operate the railway a Hornsby-Ackroyd oil engine was preferred to steam owing to the cost of supplying water for a boiler at such a height. The engine was housed in a single-storey brick build-

24) The Steep Grade railway on the northern slope of the South Downs. (J. S. Gray)

DEVIL'S DYKE RAILWAY, BRIGHTON—ARRANGEMENT OF POWER STATION

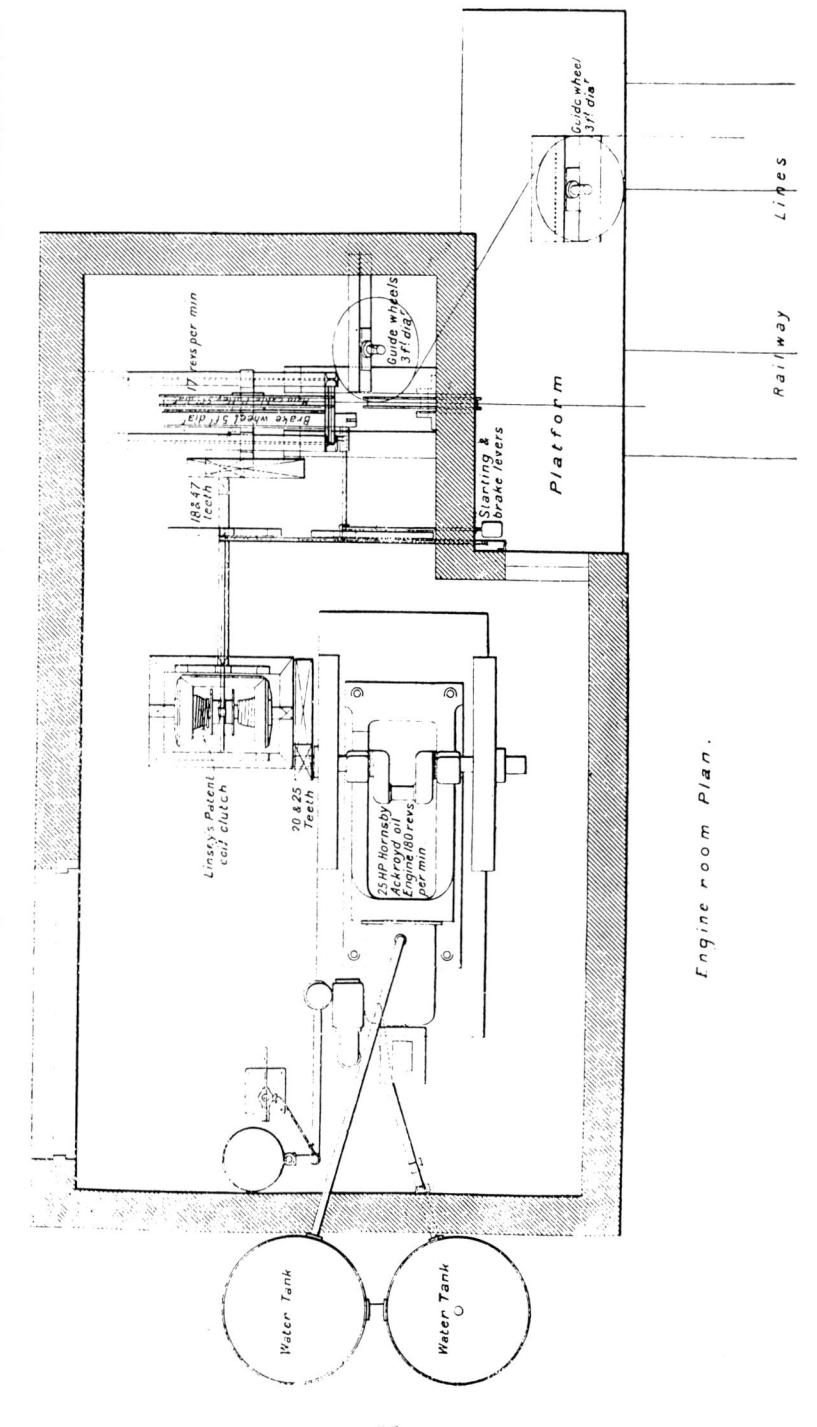

ing measuring 28ft 6in by 17ft 10in, which also served as the station, with open platforms supported on trestles surrounded by wooden fencing. The engine developed 25 b.h.p. at 180 r.p.m. and was geared down to drive a 5ft diameter pulley at 17 r.p.m. around which passed two five-eighths of an inch diameter steel cables which were lead to the main driving pulley by 3ft diameter guide wheels. Each of the 60-strand steel cables was capable of taking the full load having a united braking strain of 34 tons. This resulted in a car speed of just under 3 m.p.h. or 260ft per minute. When tension on one cable was withdrawn, four gripper brakes on the cars were automatically applied. These gripper brakes were effectively four sets of steel jaws, the shape of the grip preventing the cars from jumping the track. These brakes could also be actuated independently by hand wheels at each end of the cars. There was also a powerful brake on the shaft of the main hauling pulley worked by a foot lever from the platform, for use in an emergency. The starting and reversing gear of the continuously running engine was arranged with bevel wheels, having a Lindsay patent coil clutch for the reversing movement, which could be actuated from the platform and also used as an emergency brake.

A set of spring buffers, at a cost of £20, was provided at the lower end of the line and suitable provision, by means of electric communication, was made for warning the man in charge of the machinery at the upper station when the cars had passed a given point. A platform at the lower end was constructed of Black Staffordshire brick.

The two cars, which were constructed by the Ashbury Railway Carriage and Iron Company Ltd., were roofed and mounted on steel underframes with two feet diameter cast steel wheels. They were open above the waist rail and could seat 12 persons, a platform being provided at each end for the conductor. The entrances, by sliding door, were at each end and access to the interior was by a step gangway down the centre. The floors were at an angle of 30 degrees to the horizontal.

Construction work started early in 1897 and was completed in time for Sir Henry Howorth, M.P., to perform the opening ceremony at 3 pm on 24 July of that year. Sir Henry spoke for five minutes at the top station in the presence of a large company of shareholders and other interested persons. The sunshine that morning was, he said, a happy augury for the future of the undertaking which had been carried through with great success both by those who found the money and those who found the brains. He was sure that all present would join with him in the hope that the railway would live for very many years to add to the pleasure of visitors and to the prosperity of the villages around them.

After Sir Henry Howorth's speech came the first public trip of the cars. There were three return trips and most of the party, including Sir Henry, was carried. A report in the "Brighton Gazette" of 29 July described the journey as follows;

"The cars do not move rapidly but are kept well under control from first to last. They travel easily, and smoothly, and there is

25) The upper station and engine house. (J. S. Gray)

26) The upper station and engine house. (J. S. Gray)

an utter absence of anything in the way of sensation. The journey is certainly a curious one, but that is all. Of course it is pleasant, the cars affording a charming view of the country, and there is the further attraction of the novelty of the whole thing."

After the three journeys had been completed the company adjourned to the Hotel for a luncheon. The speeches which followed were often of a witty nature and there was great optimism for the success of the railway. Mr Pitt, one of the directors, was confident there would be a handsome dividend, and he predicted the shares would soon be worth £3 or £4 apiece. The toasts included "The Town and Trade of Brighton", "The Press", and "The Ladies". The company returned to Brighton on the 5.07 pm train. The fares charged on the new line were 2d single and 3d return.

The Steep Grade appeared to have got off to a very good start; indeed, the "Brighton Gazette" on 12 August 1897 reported that Bank Holiday was a big day for the railway, "so heavily was it patronised that the receipts were at the rate of £5 per hour. Good business."

It is interesting to examine how well shares were being sold prior to the opening. A summary of Capital and Shares for 17 February 1897 is shown below;

Number of Shares taken up		320
Called up	320	
Calls received	313	
Calls unpaid	7	
	320	

These represented eighteen shareholders including an initial seven holding £1 each. The largest shareholder was E. C. Stuart Cole, of Brighton, who held £100 worth of shares. Among the remainder were 6 Brighton grocers, a plumber from Easingwold, and a Clerk in Holy Orders, the Rev. J. H. Le Breton Girdlestone, of Bovey Tracey, Devon. Although the railway was open and running, however, all was not well with the Company. By 17 February 1899 the position was as follows;

Number of Shares taken up		1583
Called up	833	
Calls received	826	
Amount agreed to be considered as paid	750	
Calls unpaid	7	
	1583	

This sum represented thirty-nine shareholders. Matters came to a head early in 1899 when the Pyramidical Syndicate Ltd. was in the course of being wound up and a debenture holder named Annie Havers brought an action in the Chancery Division of the High Court to investigate the state of the Brighton Dyke Steep Grade

Railway Company. By an order dated 8 July 1899 this was done and from the enquiries and various affidavits rendered, it was revealed that the Company was indebted to the Pyramidical Syndicate Ltd. to the tune of £4,766.5.6. The latter claimed a lien on the lease and on 1 December 1899 gave an equitable charge on the lease to Major-General Penny of the Steep Grade Company to secure £1,000. It was most unlikely that this sum could ever have been raised and the position of the debenture holders and shareholders was, by this time, so hopeless that their best policy was to combine and form a syndicate to purchase the railway at as low a price as possible. To add to the difficulties the railway had ceased to work sometime during 1899 and to enable a sale as a going concern, a further loan was obtained to put the line in good repair, and re-open it.

A High Court Order dated 16 July 1900 directed that the railway be sold and an announcement to that effect appeared in the "Sussex Daily News" and "Brighton Gazette" on 12 December;

SALES BY AUCTION
TOMORROW
In the High Court of Justice — Chancery Division
Mr Justice Kekewich   1899   B. No. 697

In the Matter of the Brighton Dyke Steep Grade Railway Limited
—Havers v. Brighton Steep Grade Railway, Limited.

TO ENTERTAINMENT, CONTRACTORS, ENGINEERS,
SYNDICATES, SPECULATORS, etc.
NEAR BRIGHTON.
THE VALUABLE AND NOVEL UNDERTAKING,
THE STEEP GRADE RAILWAY,

Situate at THE DEVIL'S DYKE, in the Parish of Poynings, as a GOING CONCERN, including the valuable rights, concessions, stations, buildings, 25 horse power engine, hauling-gear, permanent way, cars, cables, and plant, all in good working order.

It is estimated that about 600,000 persons annually visit the Dyke and by energetic and liberal management a very large proportion of these could be attracted to use the RAILWAY, which should undoubtedly become highly lucrative and prosperous.

MR FREDERICK CECIL PARSONS,

of the firm of Messrs PARSONS and Son, with the approbation of his Lordship Mr Justice Kekewich, the Judge to whom this action is attached, pursuant to the Order therein dated 16th day of July, 1900, will sell the above by Auction, at the Old Ship Hotel, Brighton, TO-MORROW (THURSDAY), December 13th 1900, at Three o'clock precisely, in One Lot.

Solicitors: Mr C. F. Martelli, 10 Staple Inn, London, W.C.; Mr Richard Preston, Tonbridge, Kent.

Auctioneers' Offices; 163, North Street, 61, Buckingham Place, Brighton. 88, Church Road, Hove. Telephone 89.

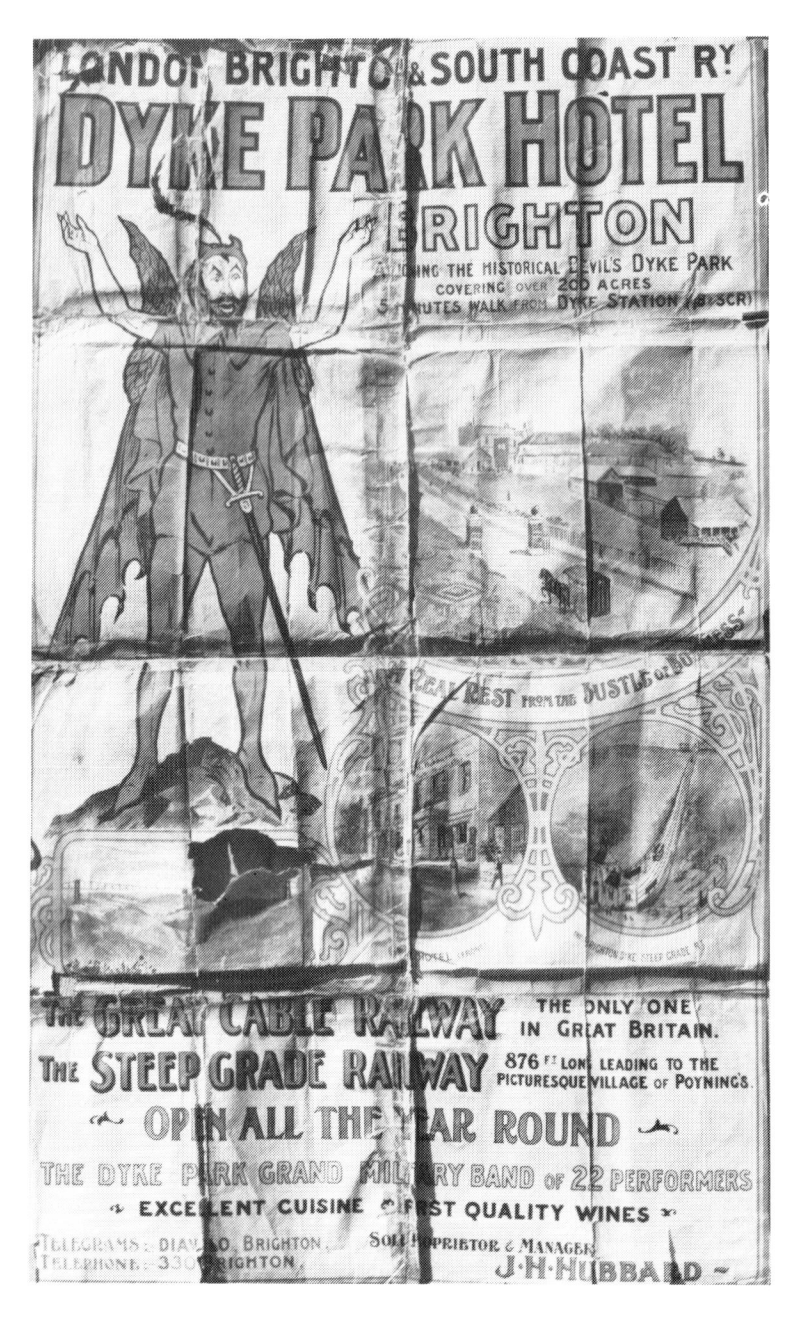

27) **Dyke Park Hotel Poster.** (P. Clark, courtesy Mrs G. Calcutt)

28) The Steep Grade railway as illustrated on the poster showing the fictitious "lower" station. (P. Clark, courtesy Mrs G. Calcutt)

In offering the property for sale the auctioneer dwelt on the opportunities which could be made, if the line was sufficiently advertised, by enterprising management. Bidding commenced at £100 but did not go beyond £390 and the property was bought in by a syndicate formed of debenture and shareholders.

One interesting sideline occurred during 1899; the Registrar of Companies persisted in writing to the offices of the Steep Grade Company, 28a Basinghall Street, demanding that returns be submitted. The letters, six in all, were all returned endorsed, "Gone away, housekeeper." The Registrar dissolved the Company by notice in the "London Gazette" dated 18 November 1902.

Meanwhile the Steep Grade Railway continued to operate but the visitors who had descended to Poynings were now being attracted to a new motor-bus service through the easier Newtimber Gap. In addition the Hotel was catering increasingly in the way of refreshment for the day visitor thus alleviating the temptation to use the line to descend to Poynings.

The dwindling traffic, coupled with the aforementioned financial problems of Mr Hubbard, contributed to an inevitable closure. The line seems to have ceased operation around 1908 or 1909, the equipment being removed around 1913.

Mrs A. Haffenden, of Henfield, Sussex, can vividly remember riding her bicycle on more than one occasion with her father and sister to the bottom of the incline and travelling up to the Dyke Hill on the Steep Grade Railway. These outings took place when Mrs Haffenden was 12, in 1905. She recalls that the car had enough room at each end to take the bicycles.

The artist of the Dyke Park Estate poster referred to in Chapter One and illustrated elsewhere most interestingly depicts an imposing building at the lower terminus of the Steep Grade Railway. This was purely an invention by the artist as there is certainly no evidence of there ever being a building on the site. Today, amongst the undergrowth which was once the lower terminus, one may discover bricks from a building, but these originated from the upper station.

CHAPTER SIX

Remains

The Dyke Hotel was gutted by fire in 1945 but was rebuilt as a restaurant in 1954.

There is very little evidence at Devil's Dyke to show there was ever a Steep Grade railway, or aerial cableway. The intrepid explorer may care to descend the plainly visible scar in the northern slope that was the Steep Grade to find wooden piles and bolts protruding from the chalk. Indeed, the foundation bricks of the upper station are still in situ. As for the aerial cableway all that remains are the two bases for the pylons on each side of the ravine.

After the closure of the standard gauge line, all buildings and equipment were removed at Rowan and the Dyke after the outbreak of the Second World War, the demolition train being hauled by C2X 0-6-0 No. 2523. Dyke Junction Signalbox was abandoned after the closure, but was not finally dismantled until it had received a fresh coat of paint! The road under the bridge at Hangleton was filled up to rail level during the War to enable Canadian tanks to transverse Hangleton Road as they were incapable of dipping down to pass under the bridge. The embankment north of Hangleton bridge was gradually chipped away after the War.

Whilst travelling between Aldrington and Portslade stations on the Brighton to Portsmouth line one can easily detect where the branch left the main line, through what is now Harrington's Garage. From there the line is buried under the Hangleton estate save a short stretch near Knoll Recreation Ground. A diligent searcher may discover the site of Rowan Halt behind Rowan Avenue and adjacent to an unusually large gap between two houses. Beyond the Downsman Public House, however, the scar is clearly visible and, indeed, it has been preserved as a public walkway. The cutting, which was filled with five feet square concrete blocks from Hove's sea defences together with hundreds of coils of rusty barbed wire, has been levelled. Golf Club Halt platform can still be found by taking a slight deviation from the walkway, which takes a different route to the railway from near the Halt to the Dyke. At the terminus itself the platform is still visible and is now part of a farm.

The wheel of the history of the Dyke railway has now turned full circle. The superb views which always provided an excuse to ride on the train are free once more — but for the willpower to make the walk.

29) The village of Poynings from the remains of the Steep Grade railway engine house in 1975. (P. Clark)

Appendix (i)

TIMETABLE AND FARES, SEPTEMBER 1887

Down Weekdays

Brighton	8.00	9.15	10.35	12.0	1.25	2.50	4.15	5.40
West Brighton	8.6	9.21	10.41	12.6	1.31	2.56	4.21	5.46
Dyke Jct. (pass)	8.7	9.22	10.42	12.7	1.32	2.57	4.22	5.47
Dyke	8.20	9.35	10.55	12.20	1.45	3.10	4.35	6.00

Down Sundays

Brighton	9.35	11.15	2.40	3.40	5.25
West Brighton	9.41	11.21	2.46	3.46	5.31
Dyke Jct. (pass)	9.42	11.22	2.47	3.47	5.32
Dyke	9.55	11.35	3.00	4.00	5.45

Up Weekdays

Dyke	8.45	9.55	11.20	12.35	2.00	3.25	5.00	6.30
Dyke Jct. (pass)	8.57	10.7	11.32	12.47	2.12	3.37	5.12	6.42
West Brighton a.	8.58	10.8	11.33	12.48	2.13	3.38	5.13	6.43
West Brighton d.	9.00	10.10	11.35	12.50	2.15	3.40	5.15	6.45
Brighton	9.5	10.15	11.40	12.55	2.20	3.45	5.20	6.50

Up Sundays

Dyke	10.25	12.00	3.10	4.30	6.20
Dyke Jct. (pass)	10.37	12.12	3.22	4.42	6.32
West Brighton a.	10.38	12.13	3.23	4.43	6.33
West Brighton d.	10.40	12.15	3.25	4.45	6.35
Brighton	10.45	12.20	3.30	4.50	6.40

All trains 1st, 2nd, 3rd class

Fares between Brighton Central (or West Brighton) and Dyke

SINGLE			RETURN		
1st	2nd	3rd	1st	2nd	3rd
1/-	9d	5d	1/6	1/2	10d

Appendix (ii) TIMETABLE AND FARES, JUNE 1912

Weekdays

Brighton	* 9.15	10.0	11.3	11.53	12.55	2.40	3.30	4.40	5.47	6.57	† 7.55
Holland Road Halt	—	10.3	11.6	11.56	12.58	2.43	3.33	4.43	5.50	7.0	7.58
Hove	9.22	10.6	11.9	11.59	1.1	2.46	3.36	4.46	5.53	7.3	8.1
Dyke Junction Halt	—	10.8	11.11	12.1	1.3	2.48	3.38	4.48	5.55	7.5	8.3
Dyke	9.38	10.20	11.23	12.13	1.15	3.0	3.50	5.0	6.7	7.17	8.15

Sundays

Brighton	10.0	11.0	11.53	2.40	3.35	4.30	5.30	6.25	7.25	*† 8.30
Holland Road Halt	10.3	11.3	11.58	2.43	3.38	4.33	5.33	6.28	7.28	—
Hove	10.6	11.6	12.1	2.46	3.41	4.36	5.36	6.31	7.31	8.35
Dyke Junction Halt	10.8	11.8	12.3	2.48	3.43	4.38	5.38	6.33	7.33	—
Dyke	10.20	11.20	12.15	3.0	3.55	4.50	5.50	6.45	7.45	8.50

Weekdays

Dyke	* 9.50	10.33	11.28	12.25	1.35	3.5	4.15	5.10	6.15	7.25	†† 8.25
Dyke Junction Halt	—	10.44	11.39	12.36	1.46	3.16	4.26	5.21	6.26	7.36	8.36
Hove	10.5	10.46	11.41	12.38	1.48	3.18	4.28	5.23	6.28	7.38	8.38
Holland Road Halt	—	10.48	11.43	12.40	1.50	3.20	4.30	5.25	6.30	7.40	8.40
Brighton	10.12	10.52	11.47	12.44	1.54	3.24	4.34	5.29	6.34	7.44	8.44

Sundays

Dyke	10.30	11.30	1.5	3.5	4.0	4.55	5.55	6.50	8.0	*† 9.0
Dyke Junction Halt	10.41	11.41	1.16	3.16	4.11	5.6	6.6	7.1	8.11	—
Hove	10.43	11.43	1.18	3.18	4.13	5.8	6.8	7.3	8.13	9.14
Holland Road Halt	10.45	11.45	1.20	3.20	4.15	5.10	6.10	7.5	8.15	—
Brighton	10.49	11.49	1.24	3.24	4.19	5.14	6.14	7.9	8.19	9.19

All trains Motor except those marked * which were 1st/3rd (mixed train)
† (not September)
†† (not September; Mon./Wed./Fri. in June/July/August runs 35 mins. later)

Appendix (ii) — continued

JUNE 1912 Special Rail Motor Fares

To/From Dyke	Holland Rd Halt	Dyke Jct. Halt
	5d	4d

Season ticket rates

Brighton–Dyke (Third class)

Annual	6m	3m	2m	1m
£5.17.0	£2.18.6	£1.9.3	£1.4.3	14.9

Appendix (iii) TIMETABLE, NOVEMBER 1938

Down Weekdays

HOUR	6	6	7	8	9	10	11	12	12	2	3	4	5	6	S	E		Down Sundays
															7	7	8	10 11 12 1 2 3 4 5
Brighton	42	14	42	13	10	10	8	8	42	10	10	10	7	10	7	10	8 —	10 10 8 10 10 10 10
Holland Road Halt	44		44		12	12	10	10	44	12	12	12	9	12	9	12	10 —	10 12 10 10 13 12 12 13
Hove	46	17	45	16	14	14	12	12	46	14	14	14	11	14	11	14	12 —	13 14 12 12 15 14 14 15
Aldrington Halt	48		48	19	16	15	14	14	48	16	16	16	13	16	13	16	14 —	15 16 14 14 17 16 16 17
Rowan Halt	52	21	52	23	19	19	17	18	51	19	19	19	16	19	16	19	17 —	17 20 19 19 20
The Dyke						30	30	28	2	30	30	30	27					20 19 17 17 20 19 19 20
																		31 30 28 28 31 30 30 31

Up Weekdays

HOUR	7	7	8	8	9	10	11	12	1	2	3	4	5	6	7	8		Up Sundays
																		10 11 12 1 2 3 4 5
The Dyke	0	24	0	33	37	37	37	20	37	37	39	37	37				—	39 37 36 46 38 37 37
Rowan Halt	2	25	2	35	46	46	46	29	46	46	48	47	47	47	47	31	—	48 46 45 55 47 46 46
Aldrington Halt	4	23	4	37	49	49	49	31	32	49	51	50	50	50	50	33	—	50 49 48 58 50 49 50
Hove	6	30	7	40	51	51	51	33	34	51	54	52	52	52	52	36	—	53 51 50 0 52 51 52
Holland Road Halt					53	53	53	36	36	53	56	54	54	54	54		—	55 53 52 2 54 54 54
Brighton	10	34	10	44	57	57	57	39	40	57	0	58	58	58	58	41	—	59 57 56 6 58 58 58

S — Saturdays only
E — Except Saturdays

All trains one class only

Appendix (iv)
LOGS OF SENTINEL RAILBUS TRIALS
21st March 1933

		First trip			Second trip			
		h.	m.	s.		h.	m.	s.
Brighton	dep	12	46	00	dep	2	42	00
Holland Road	pass	12	48	30	pass	2	44	30
Hove	arr	12	49	30	arr	2	46	30
	dep	12	50	00	dep	2	47	15
Aldrington Halt	pass	12	52	30	—			
Junction	stop	12	53	00	stop	2	48	00 (pick up Single
		—			start	2	48	45 line Staff)
$\frac{1}{2}$ m.p.	pass	12	54	30	pass	2	51	00
$\frac{3}{4}$ m.p.	pass	12	55	15	pass	2	51	40
1 m.p.	pass	12	56	00	pass	2	52	20
$1\frac{1}{4}$ m.p.	pass	12	56	45	pass	2	53	00
$1\frac{1}{2}$ m.p.	pass	—			pass	2	53	45
$1\frac{3}{4}$ m.p.	pass	12	57	20	pass	—		
2 m.p.	pass	12	58	10	pass	—		
$2\frac{1}{4}$ m.p.	pass	12	59	00	pass	—		
$2\frac{1}{2}$ m.p.	pass	12	59	43	pass	2	56	15
$2\frac{3}{4}$ m.p. (G.C. Halt)	pass	1	00	25	pass	2	56	35
3 m.p.	pass	1	01	00	pass	—		
$3\frac{1}{4}$ m.p.	pass	1	01	30	pass	2	57	55
The Dyke	arr	1	02	15	arr	2	58	45
					(20 passengers taken)			

Water used 40 gallons · · · · · · Water used 40 gallons

		First ret. trip			Second ret. trip		
		h.	m.	s.		h.	m.	s.
The Dyke	dep	1	8	30	dep	3	6	00
$3\frac{1}{4}$ m.p.	pass	1	9	45	—			
3 m.p.	pass	—			pass	3	7	45
$2\frac{3}{4}$ m.p. (G.C. Halt)	pass	1	10	45	—			
$2\frac{1}{2}$ m.p.	pass	1	11	27	—			
$2\frac{1}{4}$ m.p.	pass	1	11	55	—			
2 m.p.	pass	1	12	30	—			
$1\frac{3}{4}$ m.p.	pass	1	13	05	—			
$1\frac{1}{2}$ m.p.	pass	1	13	25	—			
$1\frac{1}{4}$ m.p.	pass	1	14	15	—			
1 m.p.	pass	1	14	52	—			
$\frac{3}{4}$ m.p.	pass	1	15	38	—			
$\frac{1}{2}$ m.p.	pass	1	16	30	—			
$\frac{1}{4}$ m.p.	pass	1	17	08	—			
Aldrington Halt	pass	1	18	15	pass	3	16	30
Hove	arr	1	19	40	arr	3	18	15
	dep	1	20	15	dep	3	18	45
Holland Road Halt	pass	1	21	45	pass	3	20	00
Brighton	arr	1	24	00	arr	3	22	15

Water used 15 gallons · · · · · · Water used 23 gallons

Appendix (v)

RECEIPTS OF BRIGHTON AND DYKE RAILWAY 1913

Extracted from "Southern Railway Company — Published Financial Accounts and Statistical Returns of the Companies Forming the Southern Railway Company (as per Railway Act, 1921) For the Year 1913."

Revenue Receipts and Expenditure of the Whole Undertaking:

	Receipts	Expend.	Net. Receipts
Coaching traffic	872 17 5		
Goods traffic	7 6 10		
	880 4 3		
Land tax	3 4 2		
Printing etc. of warrants	2 4 4		
		5 8 6	
	880 4 3	5 8 6	874 15 9
Total Net Income — £874 15 9			

Proposed Appropriation of Income:

Balance B/F from last year's a/c		DR208 17 5
Net Income 1913		874 15 9
		665 18 4
Deduct:		
Interest on Debenture stock	960 0 0	
General Interest	13 10 10	DR973 10 10
	BALANCE:	DR307 12 6